SCOTTISH BARONIAL HOUSES

Scottish Baronial Houses

by

HUBERT FENWICK

ROBERT HALE · LONDON

Robert Hale Limited
Clerkenwell House
Clerkenwell Green
London EC1R 0HT

Fenwick, Hubert
  Scottish baronial houses.
  1. Historic buildings—Scotland
  I. Title
  941.1 DA875

ISBN 0–7090–2581–5

Photoset in Palatino by
Kelly Typesetting Ltd,
Bradford-on-Avon, Wiltshire
Printed in Great Britain by
St Edmundsbury Press, Bury St Edmunds, Suffolk
Bound by WBC

Contents

Acknowledgements

I would like to thank the Lord Lyon King of Arms for his advice on the working of the feudal system in modern Scotland, Anne Roberts for fair typing my original manuscript, and Ronald Miller of Pittenweem, whose baronial arms appear on the back cover of this book, for reading the proofs.

The sketches and photographs are all the author's except five engravings which are taken from R. W. Billing's *Baronial and Ecclesiastical Antiquities of Scotland*, first published in 1852, and the picture of Winton House on the outer cover, which was taken by Sir David Ogilvy of Inverquharity, Bart.

Illustrations

Introduction

Prompted by a recent publication devoted to English manor houses, I thought I would try my hand at a Scottish equivalent. I know the term 'manor house' does not readily conjure up anything particularly Scots nor the name 'lord of the manor' describe a Scottish laird. Yet they are nearer than might at first seem, especially if one is dealing with Caledonian barons and baronies, before the nineteenth century, and the wholesale renaming of towers, manors and halls as 'castles'. It is curious this, especially when compared with the modern habit of calling everything a 'cottage'. 'I hear you have a cottage in the country,' people say, referring, in the case I have in mind, to a three-storeyed, detached house by the sea! The Victorians obviously thought it the thing to possess a castle, and if the building in which they lived or to which they repaired for shooting or fishing was not authentically one, they were quite prepared to call it so, even to build a brand-new turreted edifice and call it Castle So-and-so. The relationship between these renamed *châteaux* and anything genuinely baronial was often remote and rarely existed at all in the case of new mansions, however much turreted and battlemented. It is true that Balmoral, perhaps the most celebrated of these latter-day fortalices, could claim ancient feudal origins, for before Prince Albert acquired the property there was already a castle on the site, one that had been enlarged and made more comfortable inside by the former British Ambassador to Vienna, a tenant of the feudal baron.

In practice the feudal system came to Lowland and parts of Highland Scotland almost as soon as it came to England. Indeed, many Norman families had already settled in the north before William the Conqueror arrived in England, and by the twelfth century Queen Margaret and her sons had formally introduced the rule of monarch, Church and barons into their kingdom. In the first instance, of course, a baron was not a titled person as today, in the House of Lords, or its medieval version, but the

King's chief tenant, an officer of the law acting on behalf of his royal master and answerable to him for most things. He had the power of *fossa et furca*, pit and gallows, the male delinquent being hanged from the fork (*furca*) of a sycamore tree and the female ducked in the ditch (*fossa*) of the manor house. One is reminded of the, possibly apocryphal, story of the youth who showed some natural reticence at going to the gallows being encouraged by his mother with the words: 'Come on now, Davie, and be hangit, and don't annoy the laird.' As late as the time of the Reformation they were ducking not only witches but religious statues, just for good measure!

In return for their lands and privileges the barons owed the king personal service in war and during civil disturbances, bringing with them their vassals or bondmen. This included regular practice at the butts with the bow; absence or playing at football or golf resulted in a fine which went to provide refreshment for those who did attend these wappinschaws, or 'territorial' exercises. Later on the service became less irksome and eventually merely a formality, the 'reddendo' sometimes being reduced to a nominal 'penny' to be paid to the king annually, or, as in the well-known case of the Clerks of Penicuik, whose motto is 'Free for a Blast', a toot on the horn whenever the monarch appeared in the barony. The latter was a complete unit, with mill, brewery and forge, in the upkeep of which all had a part. In fact, even the morals and health of vassals became the concern of the baron and the community as a whole, and excess drinking, for example, was punished by fines. A great deal of this is not dissimilar from conditions in England, nor is the nomenclature very different either.

Most original documents relating to Scottish baronies refer to them variously as *castelli* or *maneris*, and the majority possessed no castle at all but the baron's manor house whence justice was dispensed. Indeed, until the mid-fifteenth century, when King James 'of the Fiery Face' granted certain subjects the right to build stone towers and to fortify them, all castles were either royal or built at the king's discretion. A typical one was at Drum, in Aberdeenshire, where the old stone tower dates from the reign of Robert the Bruce and is the most ancient remaining entire, and used. It was built by the Irvines, lords of the manor and feudal barons in their capacity as guardians of the Royal Caledonian

Forest.

Practically the only other stone buildings of the period were those of the Church, and that is why the oldest roofed and habitable manor in Scotland is Provan Hall, on the outskirts of Glasgow, which was the property of a prebend, or canon, of St

Pittenweem Priory, showing Prior's lodging, gatehouse and kirk

Mungo's Cathedral and escaped damage at the Reformation through being secularized in time. Pittenweem Priory, or Prior's Hall, though enlarged and altered internally down the ages, has also survived, having been continuously occupied since the thirteenth century as 'the Manor House of Pittenweem'. It has been the seat of both spiritual and temporal barons, the present one displaying on his Coat of Arms and banner the figure of St Adrian, who founded the original priory in the ninth century.

Until the ending of the two hundred years peace between England and Scotland that existed from the arrival of the Saxon Queen Margaret to that of the invading Plantagenet, Edward I, architecture and culture generally were much the same north and south of the Border. Development was parallel rather than different, and but for Edward's aggression the two countries might have become one much quicker than they did and without any of the bloodshed or political and ecclesiastical strife that preceded the eventual unions of 1603 and 1707. That there was this bloodshed and strife may be deplored, probably ought to be, but it did provide interesting and separate histories, not to mention laws and traditions, and above all a separate architecture which in Scotland became more and more Continental in feeling.

A lot has been made of the Frenchness of Scotland's architecture, yet despite appearances it was a quite natural growth, the Scots not actually copying anyone but living in a cultural environment more akin to that of folk across the Channel, and particularly of northern French and Flemish provenance. The nineteenth-century return to what was termed the Franco–Scottish style, as represented in the more effusive baronial exercises of that century, had little or nothing to do with this earlier period. They were not even truly imitative, though their perpetrators may have thought they were, only the inventions of a would-be romantic age, created not for feudal barons but for the new rich and the newly ennobled. Strictly speaking they are out with this survey but have to be mentioned briefly in order to avoid confusion. What really happened in the late Middle Ages in Scotland was that turrets and round towers, tall roofs and other supposed 'French' features were the norm, as in most European countries, and it was mainly in royal palaces and larger buildings whose owners had direct links with France that conscious franco-philia ruled.

It will be seen that the differences between English and Scottish manors and baronies, at the beginning and to some extent until comparatively modern times, are less than might have been thought, and more in detail than in practice. Scotland is a very homogeneous country and like most small states adjoining larger and more powerful ones has clung tenaciously to those things it considers its own, its legends, its cultural traditions and tribal peculiarities, but as far as this survey is concerned it is the visual differences that are the more important. In England, for instance, the average manor house is in the midst of a village complex, with church, vicarage and pub nearby, while in Scotland this situation scarcely existed before the eighteenth century, and the virtual ending of feudalism in the old sense. The first true village in Scotland was Gifford, in East Lothian, which was planned as an entity when the ancient baronial seat was exchanged for a Palladian mansion. It is a 'model village', with church at one end of the street, pub half-way down and mercat (market) cross at the other. More often a Scottish village was a scattered assembly of buildings occupying far corners as well as the centre, with no cosy relationship between manor house, church and inn, all of which might be separated by as much as a couple of miles or more.

Apart from such obvious differences as the above there were, naturally, others of a more profound and particular kind. In the first place it was not Anglo-Saxon civilization that the Normans had to adapt north of the Border but something much deeper rooted and more integral, namely Celtic culture, whether Pictish or Scots. In fact, the Scots had hardly conquered the Picts, more perhaps through miscegenation than in battle, than the Saxon Margaret, fleeing from invading Normans in the south, married the last Scoto-Pictish king, Malcolm Canmore, and began the process, ironically enough in the circumstances, of romanizing the Celtic Church and feudalizing the secular government. This feudalizing was fairly easy in the Lowlands but only partially successful elsewhere, the Celtic chiefs ranking as princes and kings, and not especially susceptible to ideas from outside. When they did accept a form of feudalization, they did so largely to implement their own power and to appoint secondary barons outwith the authority of the king of Scots. At Kilravock, for example, near Nairn, on the edge of the Highlands, it was the Lord of the Isles, not James 'of the Fiery Face', who granted the Norman Rose barons their charter and the right to build a fortified tower.

In due course there did arise an interesting amalgam between the two cultures which was not wholly feudal or wholly Celtic and which lasted in some form until the failure of the Jacobite rebellions and the subsequent enacting of the Heritable Jurisdiction Act of 1748. This was mainly concerned with curbing the influence of the Highland chiefs and clans, though it did also weaken feudalism at the same time. The idea seems to have been to bring some form of conformity to Scottish institutions generally, to devitalize the clan system in particular and to reduce the power of the feudal baronage. The Act undoubtedly reduced the baron's judicial rights, but then some of these had hardly been in action for centuries; to hang a man, to duck a woman, one must have the actual means of doing so, and that had long since gone by the board.

It was once suggested to the baron of Pittenweem that, in order to stop vandals in the public park next door, he should shoot one of the miscreants and bury him under the apple tree. This advice came from a fellow baron and former convenor of the now defunct county council, and, although it may have seemed a good throw-away answer, it scarcely represented a viable proposition. On the other hand, lesser rights, such as the imposition of small fines and the putting of delinquents in the stocks were retained in the 1748 Act, so that the base of the feudal system remained intact. It might be interesting to test the legal position now by setting up some stocks in the front garden and attempting to deal with the vandals that way!

One unexpected result of the partial weakening of the power of the barons' courts, and their codification in a more general system of law, is touched on by the late Sir Thomas Innes of Learney in his book *The Scottish Clans*. Here he suggests that, had the baron's judicial powers survived *in toto*, they might have mollified the effects of the notorious 'clearances', when absentee or foreign landlords cleared the people off their land to make room for sheep. This probably had to happen sooner or later, but the point is that, by removing some of the restraints incumbent on responsible baronial administrators, landowners became little more than autocrats with nothing to deter them from doing what they liked and how, on their own estates.

There are much more significant differences and reasons for baronial survival in Scotland, as opposed to England, in the arrangement whereby the court of the Lord Lyon, northern equivalent of the College of Arms, serves as a government department with fixed duties and fees and whose pronouncements, unlike those in England, have the firm authority of law. Thus to be a feudal baron in Scotland one should have matriculated arms in the Lyon Court and have been granted a *chapeau rouge* lined with ermine and a mantle with five buttons on the right shoulder. The coat of arms was in origin literally a coat (*surtout*) which the baron wore as a form of recognition, he being known by his baronial rather than his personal name. In due course the *surtout* became a rectangular banner, which, however, should be displayed only when he himself is present and which in medieval times was often not brought out until the baron was within striking distance of his enemy. It is not a flag and should be taken down from the baronial masthead when he is out, or away, a rule which is not often obeyed. This banner represents a 'coat', minus helmet, *chapeau* and mantle, the latter now being worn on official occasions such as the opening service of the General Assembly of the Church of Scotland or the St Andrew's Day Commemoration, in which members of the Convention of the Baronage of Scotland take part. In England the red hat trimmed with ermine has been largely relegated to the inside of peers' coronets and much of the feudal heritage become little more than an amusing, if harmless, survival, like the modern cult of tartan in Scotland.

One thing the Act of 1748 did not dispose of was Feu Duties, which feudal superiors receive from their lieges, or did until quite recently, when a gradual winding-up process was inaugurated. This does not relieve a vassal from his other duties nor in any way reduce the validity of the Feu Charter between him and his superior, which may refer to the appearance of buildings, the use of land, who clears the snow away and so on. As the result of contemporary legislation Feu Duties will eventually come to an end, and the process can be speeded up by anyone who wishes to by paying off one's duty in a lump sum, as I have done. It is something akin to the English land tax, though no Scottish lawyer would say it was the same, and Scots law, like Scots religion and indeed Scots heraldry, still survives despite nearly three hundred years of joint government and more of the United Kingdom.

However, the present work is not that of either a lawyer or a herald but of an architectural historian, with most emphasis on architecture. It does not pretend to be exhaustive on the subject of Scottish feudal barons—that would be a lifetime's work. Neither does it pretend to list all the barons who have matriculated arms and possess a red hat with ermine and five-buttoned mantle. The Convention of the Baronage of Scotland list fifty or so persons as having matriculated in the past twenty years, less than half of whom live in an interesting or historic barony house, most merely possessing a field or possibly the hearthstone pertaining to such a place, for it is important to remember that the baron administered justice from his *caput*, which was not necessarily a castle or manor house but often merely the place where he flew his banner when required. There must, of course, be many barons who have matriculated before the list was compiled and many who have not matriculated at all, though they may inhabit manor houses or towers which are the *caput* of a barony—nothing like the numbers existing two or three hundred years ago, when as many as ten thousand feudal barons were recorded. Although there can hardly be a tenth of that number now, many, such as farmers and some lawyers who should know better, are unaware of the existence of their baronies, whilst quite a few baronies have disappeared under new buildings, concrete runways, all sorts of things, their metamorphoses being more or less complete. No, what this book is about is the architecture and history of existing baronial houses known to and sketched or photographed by the author.

Perhaps the easiest way to study history and the life of our ancestors is through architecture. We disappear, as do many of our more fragile possessions, but architecture survives to remind us of the past, and even when it does not survive intact, we have archaeology and all the reminders dug up by archaeologists to recreate the story.

Scottish architecture as such did not arrive until after Bannockburn and the setting-up of a separate Scottish nation, deliberately different from the English, Welsh and Irish and joining up with its neighbours again only after a long and dour process. Before Bannockburn there was a Norman kingdom, almost a sub-kingdom, but that is a touchy point and one of the principal causes of the above-mentioned separateness. The fact is that, if Edward I of England had not wished for formal recognition of a state that already existed in practice, and demanded a public act of fealty by the king of Scots for his whole realm and not just his estates in the south, then the modern state of Scotland might never have come into existence. Certainly its individual architecture would not have developed as it did.

Norman Scotland was scarcely at all different, except in the Highlands and remoter regions, from Norman England or France or anywhere else, and thus it remained until the end of the thirteenth century, when Alexander III of Scots died without a male heir and his granddaughter was drowned returning home from Norway to claim her inheritance. Edward I was called in, by Bruce and indeed nearly the whole Norman hierarchy, to decide which of the five remaining claimants had the best right to the Scottish throne. He chose John Baliol, the correct choice as it happens, but then proceeded to try to make Baliol a mere puppet and to rule Scotland through him. In due course even the puppet resisted, and the rest of the story is well enough known. Almost the entire Norman establishment north of the Border turned on their southern 'liege lord' and finally won freedom for themselves and their land on Midsummer Day 1314 on the field of Bannockburn.

So much for history, but necessary history if one is to understand how or even why there is a separate Scottish culture and in particular a separate Scottish architecture. The late Nicolas Pevsner once declared there to be little difference between the buildings of England and Scotland, the mere addition of a few turrets and minor details like that. (Since then, of course, the Pevsner series of books on British architecture has moved north, and the first volume, *The Lothians*, appeared posthumously in 1978, with others on the way.) Had Dr Pevsner been referring to the period between, say, the end of the eleventh century and the beginning of the fourteenth, he would have been more or less right. That was when the feudal system was set up, with hundreds, running to thousands, of baronies being established by the Crown, each one with its *caput*, services, rights and privileges. The feudal barons were not the great barons as such, not the powerful arbiters of the Scots' fate but the civil servants of Norman times, their manor houses sometimes fortified but not huge castles—more like the modest seats of latter-day gentry than of the aristocracy.

Nor many such manors survive in Scotland today, none inhabited except in the case of a few of religious origin, for these were built of stone and were not demolished or seriously damaged in the wars as many secular edifices were. Some of these were not even built of stone, but of timber. Of the stone survivals the most extensive, and that difficult of comprehension at a glance on account of its scattered scantiness, is Hailes, in East Lothian. It was a true manor house, not a castle, though with defensive features at the entrance, and was built by a Norman family with similar headquarters in Northumberland. It might have survived had it not stood in the way of Cromwell's artillery nearly five hundred years after its building. Nothing else of note survives from before Bannockburn of this nature, and we have to look to the fourteenth century and beyond for inhabited or well-preserved baronial houses, many once the homes of priors and abbots who were also feudal barons.

I have mentioned Drum Castle, in Aberdeenshire, which uniquely dates from the reign of Robert Bruce and was built for the King by the Irvines as Guardians of the Royal Caledonian Forest. It is a plain, battlemented tower and not yet sufficiently different from others elsewhere to warrant the name Scottish. I have seen others very similar in northern England—at Halton, for instance, where, of course, they suffered as much from local lawlessness as the Scots did. These towers, on the other hand, do have a special connotation here for they are the prototypes of the numerous pele towers that appeared on both sides of the Border in the fifteenth century and which succeeded original wooden peles, or palisades. They are miniature Norman 'keeps' and were adapted by later generations as the basis of the Scottish tower house, that peculiarly native structure which in turn developed into the turreted Scottish castle of the Jacobean period. This latter was a purely domestic creation, though provided with decorative defensive features, and represents Scotland's most individual and finest contribution to European architecture.

The Scottish tower house is a northern form of manor house, and most examples are contemporary with the creation of the less fearsome English versions of the same type of baronial dwelling. Apart from the development of the tower house, Scottish architecture followed no logical line, foreign wars and internecine strife saw to that, and even in the case of the tower houses themselves progress was slow and fitful. In fact, three-quarters of them were built towards the end of the sixteenth century and during the first half of the seventeenth—this despite the ending of the Norman hegemony at Bannockburn in the fourteenth century, and the granting of royal permission to private persons to erect fortified stone towers in the early fifteenth.

While the English were deserting their castles and building manor houses, the Scots were still living in fortified dwellings, right up to the time of the Civil War, when Coxton Tower, at once the most perfect development from a Norman keep in the north and the last of its kind, was built. It is square, with miniature crenellated battlements and conically capped bartisans, or corner turrets, the very model of its type, and was originally entered from the first floor by a movable ladder. (All very much like the stereotyped sketch of a border keep I use as the heading to my notepaper, a conjectural Fenwick Tower.) The lower chamber served for the herding of cattle and as storage, the succeeding

Conjectural sketch of Fenwick Tower

vaulted rooms, one above the other, reached via a spiral stairway within the thickness of the walls. Coxton is built entirely of stone, roof not excluded, for at that time Scotland was short of timber, and only towards the end of the seventeenth century was the position improved, when the countryside was so planted with coniferous firs that contemporary commentators thought it looked like Norway. Coxton is also harled, which form of rough-casting had by then become well established. Fenwick Tower certainly was not; indeed, even Scotstarvit, Coxton's nearest rival as to date, is built of ashlar, or smooth, regularly coursed masonry. It has neither battlements nor other defensive features but does boast a small projecting nib within which the stairs rise, a form more typical of the average tower house as it grew from the old square keep form.

In my narrative I have described and illustrated Coxton, Scotstarvit and Amisfield, the latter almost on the English Border in Dumfriesshire and yet not built till the beginning of the seventeenth century, after the Union of the Crowns. Its varied collection of defensive devices, shot-holes, projections from which boiling oil could be thrown on unwanted visitors, grim little turrets and tiny windows was already out-of-date when created. Also interesting is the fact that Amisfield, so near England, should be so different from its neighbours across the Border and yet so like contemporary buildings in the far north of Scotland. The homogeneity of the northern kingdom could not be better demonstrated, for this tower possesses most of the martial features of say, Craigievar, in Aberdeenshire. However, they are not only purely decorative but were meant to be.

The Scots were the last people in Europe to live in castles, at least fortified dwellings such as tower houses, though curiously enough the three examples mentioned are no longer inhabited and Coxton itself may never have been, except possibly by a gardener. One must, of course, distinguish between castle and tower, the situation in Scotland being rather akin to that in France, where they do still live in castles (*châteaux*), hardly any of which were defensive in origin though developed from more genuinely warlike specimens from the Gothic era. They retain moats and towers, tall roofs and outer defences, turning such features into accepted architectural forms which have survived the centuries. Even Vaux-le-Vicomte, the last truly French *château* as opposed to a classical mansion, is surrounded by water and entered over bridges. On a massive scale and the precursor of Versailles, it evolved from medieval precepts to herald the triumph of the Renaissance much as Scottish tower houses and Jacobean castles did, though on parallel lines, not in imitation.

One of the earliest fortified stone dwellings erected under James of the Fiery Face's dispensation of the mid-fifteenth century, albeit having its charter from the Lord of the Isles, is Kilravock, already mentioned. It is square and rudely simple, with minimal fenestration, and its only projecting feature is a crenellated cap-house leading onto the battlements. This is very much a latter-day Norman 'keep' and was added to afterwards to make a more comfortable baronial house. Almost contemporary but considerably more sophisticated is Inverquharity, in Angus, former seat of the family of Sir David Ogilvy of that Ilk. It is built of beautifully coursed red sandstone, handsomely battlemented

Fifteenth-century tower house at Inverquharity

and provided with a splendid little cap-house, this one, however, not battlemented but topped with a pitched roof. Thus we see the beginnings of a tower house in the traditional mould. Much more interesting is the fact that, until demolished, probably for building materials, in the eighteenth century, Inverquharity sprouted a wing, not a mere nib for the stairs but a genuine addition with rooms in it, making its plan L-shaped. Its new owners, rather than guess what this wing might have looked like, recently rebuilt it as a Jacobean house, while providing a lift and adapting part of the old 'keep' as living-quarters.

Between the dates of Kilravock and Inverquharity there is quite a gap before the full development and burgeoning of towers and small baronial castles that occurred towards the end of the sixteenth century. Religion may be blamed for much of this delay, religion which also nearly brought the arrival of the Renaissance style into Scotland to a halt in the following century, when Wintoun Castle (now called Winton House) in East Lothian, was built with features derived from southern English sources. These came to Scotland largely through the influence of the Union of the Crowns and the movement of the Court and noble patronage south. The same explanation is valid for the entry into the country of the full Palladian style at the Restoration, when William Bruce, sharing with the 'Merry Monarch' a birthday and the same Scottish ancestors, was appointed Surveyor to the King, for whom he rebuilt the Palace of Holyroodhouse.

Bruce had served on the Secret Council that met in Holland to arrange with Charles II his return to Britain and was related to the Duke of Lauderdale's powerful and scheming wife, Bessie Dysart. This extraordinary woman, who combined the arts of witchcraft and physical beauty so successfully, at first made herself amenable to Oliver Cromwell, before turning to the King and finally to Lauderdale. The latter became the veritable 'viceroy' of Scotland, ruling the country until the ascendancy of the King's brother, James, Duke of York, whose cruelty to the Covenanters was a factor in causing his expulsion.

Sir William Bruce was the first professional Scottish architect; that is, unlike his successor and early apprentice William Adam, he was neither builder nor builder's merchant but drew plans and saw them executed in the modern manner. Before he rebuilt Holyroodhouse he had received the all-important commission to render the old Border seat of the Duke of Lauderdale fit to house Bessie, whose own mansion at Ham, near Richmond, was one of the finest and most fashionable venues of Restoration England. What Bruce achieved at Thirlestane was a remarkable *tour de force*, converting an embryo Border pele into a Renaissance baronial mansion, yet without removing the former or seriously diluting its essential character. In this exercise he more or less invented the Scottish Baronial style which David Bryce and others took hold of two centuries later but without, unfortunately, displaying Bruce's feeling and patrician taste. Bruce himself may possibly have been influenced by what Lord Dunfermline, Chancellor to

James VI and I, had done at Fyvie, in Aberdeenshire, where two separated towers were linked with a central trumphal arch. The King's Surveyor adopted this way of giving Thirlestane symmetry, and even at Holyrood he repeated it.

The disjuncture, so to speak, of many Scottish castles and

Fyvie Castle, Aberdeenshire, with Seton centrepiece

towers was a curious feature. One thinks of the Place of Mochrum, in Galloway, which was restored by the then Marquis of Bute in the late nineteenth century in what must surely be authentic manner. Here a keep-like tower, possibly of the fourteenth century but mostly of the fifteenth, stood some distance away from the later, Jacobean house. They lacked any visible junction until that necessary adjunct was provided in the restoration by a single-storeyed entrance hall. This separated towers and houses idea marks a rather different progression in the development of the Scottish tower house, an alternative to the wings at one side and small penthouse on top.

Huntingtower, near Perth, provides another well-known specimen in which the distance between two disparate towers was only nine feet before their joining. Traquair, however, is the best example of continuous development sideways rather than upwards. It dates from the fourteenth century, when a small hunting lodge was erected at what is now the northern end of a building which has been improved and extended until the second half of the seventeenth century, when James Smith, Bruce's successor as Surveyor to the King, systematized, if one can use such a word, the different parts. He also laid out a formal garden and terrace with ogee-roofed gazebos, as was the fashion at that

Entrance lodges and gates to Kinross House

time. Traquair has hardly been touched since then and claims to be the oldest inhabited house in Scotland. It is not really a tower house like the others, though it may be three tower houses in one. Its tall roofs, graced by attractive pepperpot turrets, recall the manor houses of Normandy but, in common with so many such Frenchnesses in Scotland, came to its present state quite fortuitously, none of its known builders ever having been to France.

Perhaps it was due to his royal descent, certainly to his love of country, that Sir William Bruce never entirely gave up the native idiom in architecture. Although keen on the Palladian style, Italian in provenance and just as foreign to Scotland as to England, he never adopted it at the expense of the Scottish tradition. That is why he was so successful at Thirlestane and Holyrood, where, despite his repetition of a sixteenth-century wing to produce the required symmetry, he also introduced for the first time north of the Border the three classical orders of architecture, Doric, Ionic and Corinthian, in the courtyard.

More in the present context is Bruce's own house, at Kinross, which in its day was considered the finest country mansion in Scotland and one of the most consummate essays in the Palladian architecture in Great Britain. Daniel Defoe thought so, anyway, and he was surely right. Yet, notwithstanding its grace and charm, symmetry and Italianate manner, the stables, which were begun and completed before the house had risen to the first floor, are purely vernacular, with ogee-roofed pavilions at the corners, a circular doocot (dovecote) at the centre and such local features as swept dormers lighting the attics of attendant cottages. The architect also had his garden and park laid out and planted some years before anything else was done, his son being sent to France to be 'finished' and bringing back with him hundreds of seeds from the Ile de France. Kinross is approached and surrounded by formal plantings like a French *château* and has a vista from its salon opening onto the island and castle of Loch Leven, whence Mary, Queen of Scots, escaped. It was this kind of association which seemed uniquely important to the Palladian Bruce, for his house stood in the barony of Loch Leven, whose arms he brought from the old castle and erstwhile *caput* and used as a keystone in one of his new garden gazebos.

William Adam, the last genuinely Scottish architect, genuine in the sense that his experience and practice was entirely Scottish based and not inspired by travel abroad, is said to have been apprenticed to Bruce at Hopetoun House in the first decade of the eighteenth century, though if so he was still in his teens. In any event, he and his sons worked at Hopetoun from then until the end of the century, gradually removing any sense of gentlemanly reticence that the former King's Architect had created there and making instead a huge Baroque palace which is today sold to the public as 'the Versailles of Scotland'. Hopetoun is obviously outside the present work, at least in its details and scope, but it is worth a visit, if only to see how the Bruce bit, at the back, is quiet and in keeping with the character of a Scottish barony house, perfectly proportioned and well composed in the classical manner.

Bruce was of the old school and supported the *ancien régime* in religion and politics, so he had to retire on the departure of the Stewarts to whom he had been devoted and to whom he had owed his progress in the world. William Adam was of the new régime and attached himself to the Whig ascendancy in Church and State, building houses for wealthy lawyers and politicians and for the new Civil Service. He was not a professional architect as the RIBA would define the term, owning, amongst other

Adam's grandiose Baroque 'Keep' to Duff House

things, tileworks, coalmines and breweries and running his own building concern. He owed his knowledge of the 'Mistress Art' partly to the example of Bruce but mostly to patrons such as Sir John Clerk of Penicuik, who at an early age had made the 'Grand Tour', under his own steam, and who became a considerable connoisseur before he was twenty. He later employed William Adam on his house at Mavisbank, near Edinburgh, and took him south when he visited friends there. Adam was particularly impressed by the works of Sir John Vanbrugh, playwright turned architect, which interest can clearly be seen reflected in the façades of Hopetoun and Duff House, Banff, where an unimaginative 'keep' plan, square and with turrets at the corners, is draped in elaborate Baroque ornament clearly derived from Castle Howard. The plan may also derive from Vanbrugh's scheme for a rebuilt Inveraray Castle, in Argyll, a scheme that was not begun until many years later, when William Adam acted as Master of Works with his sons in attendance.

The Adam family, William, John and Robert, with James and a younger William coming on behind, was employed by the Board of Ordnance and did valuable work for both themselves and the

Robert Adam's fort-like Seton Castle

nation repairing and building forts in the Highlands. Some of these, such as Fort George, served as barracks for Highland regiments until modern times, but more importantly they gave Robert Adam, the real genius of them all, a taste for military architecture which was to be significant, especially after he had been to Italy and studied medieval Italian castles such as Bolsena and Bracciano, in the Roman Campagna. These attracted him as much as the antiquities he dug up with Charles Clérisseau in the Roman Forum or explored in Dalmatia under the eye of the Venetian Governor, a Scotsman. This information, added to his knowledge of British military architecture, became the basis of his famous castellated style, which was unique in Europe. Only Scotland could cradle its birth, providing the proper setting for a style which was romantic in the true sense of the word, not in the Gothic Revival sense. Followers of that mode merely clothed classically planned buildings in pseudo-medieval garb. Robert Adam, on the other hand, massed his forts and castles as they might have been in Gothic times, leaving form and materials to supply the main interest. Culzean, in Ayrshire, is his most celebrated, but there are many others, including Seton, near Edinburgh, in which Italian medieval features combine with more local military sources and vernacular borrowings, such as crow-stepped gables, to produce a style that is virtually unrivalled and marks the climax of the architect's career.

Robert Adam left his native land early and seemed not to want to return there, yet it was in Scotland that he built his Renaissance forts; indeed, he showed a strange love of country that can perhaps be matched by that of Bruce, at least at the end of the day. He became a feudal baron, was Sheriff of Kinross and restored the ruins of Dowhill Castle, on the Blair Adam estate, thus, surely, emulating to some extent his great predecessor. His last neo-classical house, the modest Newliston, is also near Edinburgh, for which city he had designed Charlotte Square and a new University, neither, alas, completed as he planned or in his lifetime.

Ian Lindsay, in whose baronial house at Houstoun I once worked, and who became the principal post-war expert on historic buildings in Scotland, initiating the official grading system, used to say there was a sort of 'apostolic succession' of architect in Scotland. I don't quite remember if it went all the way back to Sir William Bruce and the Adam family but it undoubtedly pertained to the nineteenth century and twentieth. It included William Burn, whose Jacobean revival style was quite individual and greatly at odds with his almost Spartan neo-Greek alternatives. The old manor house at Tyninghame, in East Lothian, is one of his most successful and typical essays, in which he combined Renaissance detail with Gothic to create a new and grander kind of country house which, like Robert Adam's castellated buildings, was not fully understood by his contemporaries. Another in the architectural succession was David Bryce, whose baronialization of old and new buildings was progidious, though rarely sensitive. He was a master of pseudo-Gothic and neo-Baroque alike and, despite standardization of materials and details, showed considerable skill on occasion. The re-castellation of Blair after it had been reduced in height and turned into a Georgian country house in the eighteenth century is a case in point. Here Bryce emulated both Bruce and Lord Dunfermline in providing a new centrally placed arched feature, the result looking quite natural.

As I was both an assistant to Ian Lindsay and subsequently the last chief assistant in the office of Lorimer & Matthew, I think I may claim to be in the 'succession' myself, though where it has gone since I don't know. Sir Robert Lorimer was long since dead before I arrived, but the office was still concerned with his former works and interests. We designed and had made heraldic beasts and crests for Knights of the Thistle, to put above their stalls in St Giles', and undertook many other interesting ploys, such as repairs and alterations to houses and churches with which the great man and his office had once been associated. In fact, I completed a commission at Galashiels, in the Borders, which required some rather specialist and traditional stonework. For this I went to the original mason, then in his eighties, who told me how, when only seventeen years of age, he had been invited by Lorimer to come to Edinburgh with others and carve something for him to see; that was how he began his career as a sculptor, working on the Thistle Chapel. Craftsmanship was Lorimer's forte, his restorations and indeed his work generally being most successful when he stuck to what was known to be good and worthwhile in the Scottish tradition. Bryce was often only a craftsman on paper; machine-tooled masonry and pitch-pine woodwork were part of his stock-in-trade. As with many Victorians, he was more interested in the overall effect than anything else.

David Bryce was no Viollet-le-Duc, his French counterpart, who studied medieval architecture closely and whose thesis was that the Renaissance could be ignored and architectural evolution picked up again from the end of the Gothic Age. In this context he created new structures and new ways of building which were directly derived from the medieval but using more modern techniques. His best-known restoration was the huge *château* at Pierrefonds which he rebuilt for Napoleon III, raising from ancient foundations the castle as it would almost certainly have been before becoming ruined. Few Scottish architects thought like this, though Sir Robert Lorimer, another in the 'Succession', probably came nearer to that concept in that, rather than copy the old when doing a restoration, he preferred to build up from it and adapt details as he went along. He has been much criticized for this and for his sometimes too whimsical taste, but he did revive craftsmanship in Scotland as no one else has done, and at a bad period. Lorimer's restoration of Earlshall, his first full-scale job, included the relaying from a ploughed field of a formal Scottish garden, which he did admirably, merging it with a more modern one, clearly derived from the ideas of Gertrude Jekyll, if not Sir Edwin Lutyens!

This book is called *Scottish Baronial Houses* but it has nothing really to do with Lorimer's, and especially not Bryce's, essays in imitative vein, nothing to do with what is usually called 'Scotch Baronial'. The latter concerns those mostly fairly large multi-turreted edifices which in the mid-Victorian and pre-Great War eras were erected all over Scotland, in the Lowlands as well as the Highlands, and which almost invariably were labelled castles. This labelling led in turn to many of the owners of genuinely old baronial houses following the fashion, which was a mistake, though happily the trend has since been reversed and many a re-named 'castle' is now once more referred to as 'The House of'.

Actually the term 'castle' is misunderstood throughout Britain. In England it is mostly used to mean a 'keep' or fortified building of some antiquity, like a *château-fort* in France; in Scotland more often it has over the past 150 years or so been freely translated to cover country houses with, or sometimes even without, turrets, genuine lairds' towers and, of course, authentic fortified dwellings of one sort or another. The remainder of Scotland's feudal nomenclature has suffered a decline, and manor houses, halls and places have largely disappeared in that form. A pity, since they usually refer to the original and correct names of such edifices. They are dotted about the country from Caithness to the Borders and are just as interesting as, sometimes more so than, many castles, often being associated with an old family which has inhabited its barony or occupied the land since the twelfth or even eleventh century. They are as much part of the cultural heritage of Scotland as anything else that has come down to us and have the added quality of representing not a myth or a legend but a continuing history which is supported by preservation, legislation and armorial law.

1. Royal and Ecclesiastical Beginnings

The Normans penetrated Scotland; they did not conquer it. Indeed, their penetration had already begun by the time they conquered England, while for some time after that they came north more as invited immigrants than anything else. Curiously enough, a good deal of this penetration followed in the wake of Margaret and Edgar Atheling, Saxon victims of the Norman ascendancy in the south. With them came even Normanized Saxons, such as the Burnards, from Bedfordshire, an ancient family now represented by the Burnetts of Leys who have been at Crathes, in Kincardineshire, since the twelfth century. Other Norman or partly Norman immigrants of note include the Anstruthers of that Ilk. Originally known as de Candela, the Anstruthers came from southern Italy to Fife in the eleventh century, when they took the territorial name of their barony, and they are still *in situ*. Thus Scotland acquired not only abbeys and cathedrals on the northern French and southern English model but also a series of splendid castles, not as in Wales, the castles of an oppressor and conqueror, but those of the king's appointed servants, feudal barons whose duty was to administer justice and maintain the economic and cultural life of their baronies in the king's name.

By the thirteenth century Scotland, which was governed by the Norman descendants of Queen Margaret, all with English earldoms and blood connections, had become virtually indistinguishable from its southern neighbour, at least in its lowland parts, and Scottish architecture had not yet developed its own peculiar forms which it was to later. This was to occur only after Edward I made the fatal error of trying to formalize by force of arms a political and cultural situation which already existed in voluntary form. Had it not been so, the Scottish barons, such as the Bruces, would not have asked him to choose a successor to Alexander III when the royal throne became vacant, nor would they have sworn fealty to him as feudal overlord. The result of his trying to force the issue, and his invasion of the country, was that the Scottish barons resisted, and there was born the modern Scottish nation, the post-Bannockburn nation we know today. It is necessary to mention this because it is little understood not only outside Scotland but also to some extent inside, where nationalist notions have tended to cloud the issue in so many fields. As far as buildings are concerned, however, from about the middle of the fourteenth to the beginning of the eighteenth century, when once more England and Scotland began to drift together in amity, Scotland looked less to the south and more to France and the Low Countries for inspiration, creating in the process an individualistic style that might never otherwise have evolved.

Of the pre-Bannockburn period not a lot of buildings have survived, especially castles, except as ruins, for it was the policy of Robert Bruce to render them useless to King Edward and to demolish most of them. Edinburgh Castle itself came in this category, and the oldest remaining stone tower there was erected by his son in the fourteenth century; the rest was of wood which could be and was burnt at the approach of the enemy. Until the mid-fifteenth century no stone towers were permitted to private individuals, barons or not, and the very few that were erected were done so on behalf of the king, such as the one at Drum, in Aberdeenshire, built on Bruce's orders by his servants the Irvines, to guard the Caledonian Forest. It is still there, still roofed and partly used as a library, though joined since to a more comfortable manor house. Even more exceptional is Hailes, in East Lothian, which though called a castle was in origin a fortified manor. It is unique in Scotland and, but for its having become, literally, 'one of the ruins Oliver Cromwell knocked about a bit', would be even more unique—that is, undamaged and habitable, which unhappily it is not, and has not been since the seventeenth century.

Hailes pre-dates the War of Independence and was built by a branch of the de Gourlay family, whose principal seat was at Aydon, near Corbridge, in Northumberland, which is not so unusual as might at first seem since the King of Scots was himself Earl of Northumberland. It says much too for the settled conditions prevailing in northern England and southern Scotland in

The romantic ruins of Hailes Castle, East Lothian

the days before Border strife, when the feudal system reigned, that Hailes could have been sited where it was and have been what it was, a perfect type of thirteenth-century manor house. It has, of course, the usual great hall and baron's private room, or solar, chapel, stables and vaults, in one of which prisoners were held prior to the baronial exercise of the king's justice. There is also an interesting entrance from the River Tyne, on whose banks the manor house stands, with a vaulted stairway leading straight from the water. Hailes can easily be seen by passing traffic on the A1, just north of East Linton, looking west towards Traprain Law, and sitting down beside the Scottish Tyne on a small rock, looking romantic in the extreme. It is, in fact, 'emergent from a shaven lawn' and 'garrulous about its history', as Ruskin would disapprovingly have remarked, and under the care of Ancient Monuments. Having survived Bannockburn and the exchange of properties that followed the defeat of the English, when those Normans who had supported Edward Plantagenet were dispossessed and replaced by Bruce's supporters, Hailes became the seat of the Hepburn family, who enlarged it and subsequently made it into a castle, or tower of defence. James Hepburn, of course, was the paramour of Mary, Queen of Scots, whom he brought to Hailes. Thus the place might have remained had it not resisted Cromwell, whose guns reduced it to what it is today, romantic but useless.

In the following century Sir David Dalrymple acquired the barony and then went to live at Whitehall, near Musselburgh, which he renamed Newhailes and where he had the ruins painted on a panel to the right of the chimneypiece in his double-cube library. Newhailes is one of the nearest large mansions to Edinburgh and little known, except for its library. The contents were recently the subject of a death duties deal, and the books went to the National Library of Scotland, leaving the shelves quite empty. A pity, and the wrong solution in any case. What should have happened, and has just happened in another similar case, at Hopetoun, in West Lothian, is that the books should have remained *in situ*, listed, and anyone who wished to consult them or even borrow them could have done so by asking, the required items being brought to Edinburgh for the purpose and taken back afterwards. Incidentally, anyone with a special interest in thirteenth-century manor houses in the north should go to Hailes's model, at Aydon, in Northumberland. It has suffered no damage down the centuries, and the last time I was there it was a farmhouse. Since then it has gone to the Ancient Monuments people, who are restoring it most expertly. It must be one of the very few complete properties in their possession, and oddly enough, within sight of it is the tower of Halton, a hundred years younger yet curiously less sophisticated than the older, feudal buildings.

With so few stone towers, and most castles of timber, practically the only stone buildings that remained intact, and generally sacrosanct—that is, until the English ravaged the Borders in the fifteenth and sixteenth centuries—were ecclesiastical in origin or use. Thus the oldest surviving manor house, roofed and habitable, is Provan Hall, near Glasgow. This was the property of Glasgow Cathedral clergy, a sort of country retreat for the prebends, or canons, who also had town houses in the cathedral precincts of which a single one, Provand's Lordship, the oldest house in Glasgow, also survives. It is a splendid little museum of Scottish furniture and historical bygones, associated with Mary,

Provan Hall, Glasgow

Queen of Scots, who is supposed to have stayed there, and James IV, her grandfather, who was one of the prebends and used to go there on 'retreat', on an act of penance for being 'art and part', as the legal term is, in the murder of his father. Both Provand's Lordship and Provan Hall became part of the barony of Barlanark and the property of a secular prebend and canon of that name; he drew the former ecclesiastical stipend and was a lawyer of repute, becoming Lord President of the Court of Session—hence the post-Reformation haleness of the buildings. Provan Hall is a pleasant little crow-stepped rectangle, with one floor and basement, dormer windows and round tower at one corner. It has a small courtyard which is entered through an arched opening with moulded panel for baronial arms, now empty. It has obviously served meaner purposes in more recent times as an appendage of a larger house nearby but has since become the property of the National Trust for Scotland, though looked after by Glasgow Corporation and destined to form the nucleus of a public park. It has been revealed rather more than before by the creation of a new motorway leading into the city from Edinburgh, and so far no particular use has been found for it.

It is a moot point as to which is the oldest inhabited house in

Prior's Hall and Manor House, Pittenweem, Fife

Scotland. Traquair in Peeblesshire advertises itself as such but has at least two rivals, Dunrobin, in Sutherland, and Pittenweem Priory, in Fife. The interesting question is really not which is the oldest inhabited house but which is the oldest continuously inhabited one. Traquair has an ancient tower, not quite as old as Drum in Aberdeenshire, which was similarly built at royal command, to guard hunting-grounds. Part of that tower, the vaulted base into which animals must once have been herded, survives, but it could never have been the home of humans at any stretch of the imagination. At Dunrobin the very core of the castle dates back to medieval times, being now invisible from outside and entirely encased within later walls, but Dunrobin is certainly a castle, ducal and grand and slightly outwith this survey. The priory at Pittenweem is a house and has always been one, having been continuously inhabited by priors and barons since its erection in medieval times. Although the inhabitants have moved up from the lower storey to higher ones, and the topmost was heightened in the late Georgian times, with later additions being tacked on to the north, it has never been empty and never had to be restored, only renovated. The foundations of earlier buildings also survive, plus a medieval gatehouse, which, however, no longer belongs to the property, having been retained by the Church authorities when the priory was sold to the present baron.

The origins of the place might almost be said to be lost in the mists of time, though a hollow in the central vaulted room, beneath the existing drawing-room, represents the erstwhile exit of a covered way from the priory to an oratory and steps cut out of the rock leading down to St Fillan's Cave, in the garden. St Fillan is himself a shadowy character, since he is 'two', a more famous Celtic evangelist who operated mostly in Strathearn, and St Fillan of Fife, who lived in the seventh century—that is, before his better-known namesake. The cave is Y-shaped with an altar in one arm, probably partly man-made, and the saint's well and desert, or retreat, in the other. He is said to have created his illuminated gospel by the aid of a light that miraculously fell over his right shoulder, but this must surely have been the opening, once used as flue for a small fire but now closed up to prevent youthful vandals gaining access to the cave. In recent years the ornaments on the altar have gone, the water from the well has been fouled, and worse things happened, mostly perpetrated by bored bairns, though not always by them. Vandalism is a world-wide problem and apparently just as bad in Communist countries as others, but boredom in Pittenweem is almost certainly caused not by deprivation of any kind but by the exact opposite, too much of everything, and not enough to do, with large sums of money handed out by parents weary of their reponsibilities. In the days of the priors it could scarcely have been quite like this!

Curiously enough, though St Fillan and his cave gave both priory and burgh their name and *raison d'être* ('Pittenweem' actually means 'the town of the cave'), it is another, no less shadowy saint whose effigy appears on the burgh and baronial arms, St Adrian, who appears variously as a bishop on the burgh arms and as a monk on medieval seals and on the arms recently granted by the Lord Lyon to Ronald Miller of Pittenweem. One feels he should know, but no one seems sure whether the saint was Hungarian or Irish, only that in the ninth century he founded a monastery on the May Isle, out in the Firth of Forth, and was killed with his companions by the Danes shortly afterwards.

In the reign of David I the monastery was re-created by Benedictines from Reading, and not long after that the whole set-up was moved to the mainland and the already existing manor house of Pittenweem occupied by the monks. Finally the Benedictines were replaced by Austin canons from St Andrews, and they remained there until the Reformation. These were not really monks, not a closed order like the Benedictines, but canons living together in one house, with servants, free to come and go and with a prior inhabiting the manor house, or so-called Prior's Hall, today still the seat of the barony, albeit under secular occupation.

Shortly before the Reformation John Rowle, the last 'baron spiritual', took the opportunity to make his peace with the new authorities, legitimized his numerous children and started selling off parts of the property. Soon a new, secular prior was appointed, the six-year-old son of James V by Mary Erskine and half-brother of Mary, Queen of Scots. Rowle accompanied her and her half-brother to France when they were sent to safety there. Then followed two Stewart priors or commendators, and then a series of barons until today, several of the local families residing in or at least owning the priory until the Jacobite Bishop Low bought it and made it his private residence. He founded a seminary in the former dormitory buildings, now a home for retired clergy, and built St John's Church, leaving the priory for 'whoever took the services at St Johns', but this clause seems to have been got round when the property and feudal rights were recently sold.

The whole of the first floor, now the drawing-room, kitchen and dining-room, was once the refectory, or great hall, with the present dining-room on a still slightly higher level denoting the position of the prior's dais; on one side a spiral stair goes down to the prior's cellar, again used for its proper purpose, while opposite to that, in a cupboard in the wall, is what was probably part of the 'preaching pulpit', the canons being read to during meals. It has been suggested that this nicely carved Gothic column might also have been one side of a large open fireplace, but where is its pair? And what a really enormous chimneypiece it must have been, too large for any existing room or rooms.

At the Battle of Bannockburn and other significant trials of force between English and Scots, Lowlander and Highlander, a number of religious and semi-religious talismans were carried before the host. These included the so-called banner of St Columba, which was kept by the monks of Arbroath and taken into battle with the abbey vassals, lead by Irvine of Drum; the Monymusk Reliquary, which was kept for six hundred years at Monymusk in Aberdeenshire and contained a bone of St Columba; and St Fillan's hand and arm bone, the arm that shed a mysterious light and which did so miraculously when housed in Robert Bruce's tent the night before his defeat of the English at Bannockburn. Mention of this mysterious light makes one think that here, perhaps, we are talking about the saint whose cave lies below the priory garden at Pittenweem, and who is said to have illuminated his Gospel by a strange light. It is said that St Columba himself was in more places than one at the same time and must, therefore, have been a composite figure. So possibly we have the same phenomenon here. It is certainly tempting to suppose so.

St Fillan's hand and arm were encased in silver, but unfortunately, although his crozier case and holy bell remain, nothing else does. The Reformers destroyed what they considered idolatrous relics before everything else, and we are lucky the Monymusk housing of St Columba's bone has survived, empty it is true but a genuine seventh-century article. The banner too has been lost or destroyed, no doubt considered superstitious like the rest. Yet what could be more superstitious and unchristian than the witch-hunting, for example, that superseded these, surely, comparatively harmless attachments? Witch-hunting was particularly vicious and thorough-going in Pittenweem, the poor victims of local fear and spite being burnt in a corner of the priory courtyard. As they were never buried, one supposes the ashes of these often completely innocent victims still lie there, not far from the surface. No doubt this gives credence to several of the ghost stories one hears about the place, though speaking from experience I do not find the old manor house and prior's lodging at all eerie. It was there long before the murder of these pitiful souls.

The Monymusk Reliquary, the oldest authentic object of its kind left to us, is shaped like a little house, something in the manner of the ones one sees in Limoges, only less ornate. It is preserved in the Museum of Antiquities in Edinburgh but went there only comparitively recently from its traditional home in Aberdeenshire. Its removal by sale is a sore point with the present feudal baron and his family, not only for its own sake but also because it was practically the only thing pertaining to pre-Reformation times at Monymusk. The priory was acquired at the end of the sixteenth century by the Forbes family, who are numerous in this part of the country and have possessed or still possess a number of interesting properties in east and central Aberdeenshire. William Forbes built the oldest remaining bit of the House of Monymusk and an old chimneypiece decorated with the three bridled bears of the family and the royal arms of James VI and I. There is, unhappily, little else of antiquity or architectural note, and a succession of owners, especially the Grants of Cullen who purchased the house in the eighteenth century, have added to and altered the building greatly, though Lady Grant, herself a Forbes by birth, says she has discovered an old print that shows some battlements and other features no longer extant.

The Grants of Cullen, in Banffshire, were Highland in origin, coming before that from Castle Grant, on Speyside, a large, decayed building in need of repair and resuscitation. They married into the Ogilvies and Findlaters along the Moray Firth and became Lowlanders, sided with the government in London against the Stuarts, received titles and honours and until quite recently did very well for themselves. Cullen House, which they inherited and enlarged, began life, like so many of the houses we have so far looked at, as an ecclesiastical adjunct. Robert Bruce founded a chantry chapel in the vicinity in which prayers were to be said 'in perpetuity' for his queen, and later the chapel became collegiate, with a provost, six prebends and two choirboys, who were housed in what is the nucleus of Cullen House. It is only one tiny corner now of a somewhat overgrown mansion, with both nineteenth-century baronial additions and Adam interiors, but has survived just the same, while inside some Jacobean painted panelling is magnificent of its kind. Since the house became empty, its furniture dispersed and the woods around felled,

Sixteenth-century tower, Cullen House, Banff

Cullen has presented a melancholy appearance, but it is hale and standing.

In the park are two splendid memorials to better ways and better taste in a magnificently virile and beautifully proportioned bridge leaping over the ravine to the south of the house, and the

Druminnor House, Aberdeen

extraordinarily Italian-looking gates to the north. The latter are said to have been designed by James Adam, but he was too young for that and they must be ascribed either to John, the elder brother, or more probably to Robert, the intermediate one, who undoubtedly did that superb bridge. It is in his Italian fortress style by which he ended the Renaissance in this country and his own career; not mock-Gothic but Italian and military in ethos.

Cullen and Monymusk are not at all the same kind of place nor in similar country, and the Grants who live at Monymusk follow much in the footsteps of the Sir Archibald who in Georgian times planted trees and turnips and generally improved his barony. Lady Grant, as I have said, is a Forbes by birth, which makes this particularly interesting since not only was it a Forbes who built the Jacobean core of the House of Monymusk and a Grant who bought it but another Grant who bought nearby Druminnor,

Forbes Arms, Druminnor House

ancient seat of the Forbes, and caused Archibald Simpson, architect of much of Aberdeen's best classical granite buildings, gently to 'Gothyckize' and enlarge. Thus the Grants stayed at Druminnor for just over a century, when it came on the market and was bought by the Hon Margaret Forbes-Sempill, sister of the nineteenth Baron Sempill of Craigievar, who restored her family to their ancient seat and did various things to it. She pulled down Simpson's work in its entirety and turned the Italian garden into a pony field, the first on the assumption she was restoring the fifteenth-century house to its original condition.

Druminnor certainly is a delightful place, and unique in its way, since it is not tall and offensive in build or appearance but long and almost barnlike and 'fortified' only at one end, where there is a bulbous stair-tower guarded by an iron yett (gate). The Forbes 'bears' are there, plus a shot-hole beside the off-centre entrance. It is unfortunate that in all the tidying up so much was removed, not just the 1815 'Gothycke' façade but the chief's tower and its erstwhile appertinences, such as brewhouse, bakery, barns and stables which would have been attached to the walls of a now non-existing courtyard and which were common to most baronial residences.

The Forbes were half-Highland and half-Lowland, as indeed is the district of Strathbogie, or Huntly, itself, on the edge of which Druminnor lies, while Pitsligo, which is in Buchan and is their chief 'country', is wholly Lowland. Craigievar, seat of the Sempills until handed over to the National Trust for Scotland, was described as a 'mountain *château*', which it surely is; but what of Druminnor? It is one of the earliest known 'palas-shaped' seats as opposed to a tall tower of defence, which was more common. It may in this respect follow what happened at Huntly, where the huge '*château*' of the Gordons has at one end a large round tower and runs away in more palatial form at the other. The Forbeses say that was copied from Druminnor. Be this as it may, there are certainly similarities inside and out, not least in the two ranges of vaulted rooms which in the case of Druminnor are not easy of arrangement for modern living.

Not long after completing her work of restoration and reduction Lord Sempill's sister was killed in a car accident. Then, one afternoon when her companion was showing visitors round, came a party of Forbeses wearing the clan tartan. Asked if they really were Forbeses and being told yes, they were offered Druminnor, to buy, and they did. So history not only repeats itself but seems to go round and round, especially when one of those Forbeses has since become Lady Grant and gone to live at Monymusk.

The entrance to Whithorn Priory, Wigtonshire

It is a far cry from the valley of the Don, with its Lowland straths to the east and Highland hills to the north, and west to the warm greenery and almost Iberian intimacy of Whithorn, in Galloway. It was here that St Ninian, Scotland's first bishop and formal missionary, came in the fourth century, while the Romans were still in command but shortly to depart. This was before the days of St Fillan or Columba or any of the Iona evangelizers and hermits and does not figure so prominently in Scottish histories. This is all wrong, of course, and in fact several tangible as well as spiritual remnants have survived, in Scotland's ancient episcopacy and in stones and monuments, for at Whithorn a Gothic arch with the arms of the king of Scots above and those of a fifteenth-century bishop inside the pend, leads to Whithorn Priory. Nothing like Pittenweem is there, and the house is much more modern, but behind, under what was once the apse of the priory kirk, archaeologists have unearthed not only some extremely ancient masonry, some of it still daubed with the white that gave the place in early times the name of *Candida Casa*, White House, but episcopal ornaments and insignia, now safely tucked away in museums.

Nothing of St Ninian's seems to have been carried into battle in latter-day Scotland, his memory apparently clouded by that of the Celts from Iona; a curious metamorphosis, incidentally, for all those mythical and semi-mythical souvenirs, though borne before a mainly Scottish army, were in the possession of Romanized monks and had become the particular symbols of a largely Norman and feudal baronage, opposed even more curiously by an assembly of Norman barons leading English and Welsh soldiers. The keepers of these religious talismans were called Dewars, some of whom managed to hang on to their charges after the Reformation into modern times, though most have now gone the same way into museums, and all minus their original essential parts.

One precious object, however, is not in that category and has to be mentioned here since it actually gives its name to an existing barony, that of Bachuil, which represents the *baculum* (staff) of a saint, Moluag, who lived in the sixth century and was a rival or competitor for conversions with St Columba. He evangelized the island of Lismore, in Argyll, and after him a tiny cathedral was dedicated in medieval times, now the parish kirk and with little remaining to show of its origins. On the other hand, the fame of St Moluag survives with his staff whose 'dewar' (keeper) is Alastair Livingstone, Baron of the Bachuil, which name the modest farmhouse he inhabits also bears, as *caput* of the barony. King Charles I granted Livingstone of Bachuil lands formerly held by the bishops of the Isles, and with them the guardianship of St Moluag's staff, which, after being temporarily on loan to the

Duke of Argyll at Inveraray Castle, is now back *in situ*.

Before leaving ecclesiastical connections for the purely secular, I must mention one or two bishops' palaces which were, and which in one case remains, both manor house and seat of a barony. Spynie is the largest of these and although ruined still

Bishop Innes's entrance to Spynie Palace

shows what a grand place it must have been, notably during the episcopate of Bishop Dunbar. He made a state visit to Rome in the early part of the fifteenth century and returned home full of ideas for embellishing his seat and increasing its luxury and taste, including an ornamental lock, with a canal to the sea, near Lossiemouth, and swans, as at Wells, ringing a bell when they wanted feeding.

Spynie is at present being tidied up by the Department of the

Environment but one can walk round and should notice the handsome, though ruined gateway built by Bishop John Innes slightly earlier; it is as consummate a work as anything north or south of the border with its finely chiselled and worked masonry and bold details. His arms are over it. (This is Innes country, as

Tower at Melgund Castle, Angus

we shall see, but strange that neither Inner House nearby nor any other grand seat which was once theirs remains so.) To see how much more sophisticated this gateway is than much of the rest of Spynie, one has only to look at the massive 'David's Tower', constructed sixty years later in answer to threats from the Earl of Huntly to dislodge him from his 'doocots'—and this when the episcopal builder was a son of Sir James Stewart, 'The Black Knight of Lorne', and Joan Beaufort, widowed consort of James I of Scots and granddaughter of John of Gaunt!

Something similar though not so large is the tower Cardinal Beaton, or Bethune, erected as a sort of status symbol a century later at Melgund, in mid-Angus. The story is that he married Marion Ogilvy before he took Holy Orders and subsequently had to find somewhere to put her when he did. If more modern respectability suggests this, one can hardly give it credence just the same, especially when priests and bishops and priors and abbots, let alone cardinals, more often than not had mistresses and nobody minded. In any case, he did build the tower, having acquired the barony from his sister-in-law, widow of a Murray of Kynynmound, the family which today is represented in the Earl of Minto whose secondary title is Lord Melgund. It is all a little complicated, or may seem so to readers south of the border. We in Scotland are always talking about relations and links between families in a way that seems to infuriate our neighbours—we are nearly as bad as the French, but in this case the links are worth mentioning and have a bearing on the present, and possibly future, of the Place of Melgund.

Materials for Melgund came from Arbroath at the behest of Cardinal Beaton in 1543, the bills of lading surviving to prove it. To his baronial status symbol the Cardinal added a 'palas', with all the refinements a prelate of the Renaissance could muster. Unhappily Melgund's glory did not last: a fine old chimneypiece hangs from the roofless gable of an upper floor, and there are other good details, but the Cardinal was murdered in his archi-episcopal castle at St Andrews in 1546.

Although the house remained hale, its last occupants were Jacobites who took fright at the approach of Government troops after the Forty-five, and left the dining-table in haste and went into exile in France. No one has lived there since and Melgund has been allowed to decay and fall into ruin. Some time ago Lord Minto's lawyers, wishing no doubt to sell the land whilst retaining both the *caput* of the barony and the source of their client's secondary title, let the farmer have everything, including any access, except for the actual ruins and a rim of a few feet all round. This romantic scene, with pigeons flying in and out, their pigeoncote having been demolished, rises from the midst of a cabbage field and there seems little chance of anyone being able to do much about it.

A friend of mine did enquire and was well received by the farmer. Indeed, a Ministry official suggested that a sizeable grant might be forthcoming for Melgund's restoration provided the whole building, including false 'keep', was done, and everything harled. As there was almost certainly no harling in Scotland

Ogee-roofed gazebos, Melville House, Fife. Compare lodges at Kinross

when Beaton built his country retreat for Marion Ogilvy, this seemed somewhat unnecessary, if not a form of vandalism, but then the official in question doubted the Cardinal's association with the building and twinned it with Carnassarie, a later episcopal retreat erected by the first Reformed Bishop of Argyll some thirty or forty years afterwards. On remonstrating over the harling my friend was told that all buildings in the Middle Ages had a covering of some sort! I think the man must have been thinking of *Candida Casa* and all those white abbeys and churches which were indeed a feature of the medieval world, being white-washed inside and out not as a form of weather-proofing but as a sign of Christian purity!

The first known harling in Scotland appears to have been in Jacobean times and is best seen in Aberdeenshire, where the magnates used it in order to simulate masonry and save materials and money in the building. The so-called castles of Mar, Midmar, or Ballogie, Muchall-in-Mar and Craigievar and the manor-house part of Drum were all so treated, though now coated with more garishly white, or even pink, harling that contrasts with the masonry in a way it never did before. Harling was certainly introduced as a domestic economy, if one can use the term in such a context, and not as a virtue in itself, which it often now is, even in the case of buildings in the care of Ancient Monuments, several of which have been defaced by it in recent years, mainly for easier maintenance but also because someone has told them it is 'traditional'.

The barony of Monimail lies inland from St Andrews and is merged today in that of Melville, at the centre of which is the handsome mansion of that name designed in the manner of Sir William Bruce towards the end of the seventeenth century. Melville was the seat of the earls of Leven and Melville who, being supporters of William of Orange, returned in triumph in 1689 and built themselves this fine country house. Until it was sold after the last war its contents had remained to a large degree as the lists of the late Stuart period showed, including furniture, curtains and napery, and a splendid *lit de parade* which is now in the Victoria and Albert Museum. At the sale Lady Victoria Wemyss bought back—yes, bought back—the dining-room furniture, with the Wemyss Swan device on the chairs, which had gone to Melville in the dowry of Anne Wemyss who married the second Lord Leven and Melville in 1691. They are now in the basement at Wemyss Castle in southern Fife. Melville became first a boys' school, when it was treated with some respect, after a brief Polish occupation during the war that did it no good, and is presently run as a home for the 'mentally handicapped'. Most of the panelling and wood carving will no doubt be either damaged or removed but one imagines that the portrait of Field-Marshal Lord Leven, the founder of the house, has been taken to safer territory.

Leven was a soldier under Gustavus Adolphus and, returning with other Scots who had fought on the Continent, offered his sword to the highest bidder. It happened to be the Covenanters and not the King. Subsequently, however, Lord Leven made his peace with King Charles I and swore never to take up his sword against him again. Within a year he had done so, but then recanted once more, and in his old age he trudged through the snow from Perthshire to the Borders to offer his services to Charles II as an ordinary soldier. He was taken prisoner at Dunbar in 1650, sent to the Tower of London and reprieved only through the personal entreaty of Queen Christina of Sweden. He lived to witness the Restoration of 1660 but died a year later, after justifying himself and saving the honour of his family and other mercenary friends in a quite remarkable manner.

The old tower of Monimail, which is still roofed, though used only as a superior garden house, was the retreat of the bishops of St Andrews. Cardinal Beaton came here often and caused the refined top part of the tower to be crowned with an elegant

Monimail Tower, Fife

parapet and decorated with Renaissance roundels. The workmen probably came from Falkland where they were engaged at the time on making a *château*-of-the-Loire palace out of the old Stewart hunting lodge there for James V; similar roundels and crowning features can be seen elsewhere in the neighbourhood, notably at Myres, where the Royal Claviger (Key-bearer) lived, and at Earlshall, where the work is cruder but obviously copied from original royal and archiepiscopal models. The Levens made larger windows and put attractive 'Gothycke' glass into them,

Farnell Castle, *Palatium Nostrum* of the bishops of Brechin

some of which has survived, though not perhaps the most remarkable object of all, the huge pre-Reformation pascal candle-stick from St Andrews Cathedral, which was certainly in Monimail Tower in the latter part of the nineteenth century and whose whereabouts since is in doubt.

Episcopal retreats were on the whole calmer, more secluded resorts than secular manors and, as with other religious or semi-religious property, tended to survive the vagaries of war and civil strife in a way the others did not; furthermore, they were not often adapted or made defensive. Perhaps, therefore, I might end this chapter mainly devoted to ecclesiastical baronies with a reference to one that has not only survived but is still inhabited, though not by a bishop. I refer to the *Palatium Nostrum* of the bishops of Brechin, which stands on the Kinnaird estate and has recently had a face-lift, rather more of one than its 'baron', the Earl of Southesk, intended. Again it is not a tower house, not tall but a 'palace', a term which really means long rather than high and was used for almost any distinguished secular building in sixteenth- and early seventeenth-century Scotland that was not a tower or a castle. It has some connection with the English 'place', which, according to the author of *English Manor Houses*, is less likely to represent a genuine manor than a hall. Certainly there were 'palaces' in Scotland that were not manors, some of them in towns, whereas it is unlikely that the 'House of' somewhere would be anything else, especially in the days before such nomenclature became common and even misleading.

The former bishop's palace on the Kinnaird estate is called Farnell Castle, though with what propriety I do not know. It certainly is not a castle in appearance, size or purpose. Quite modest, it displays certain unique features.

One uses the term 'unique' fairly often in Scotland because there are so many buildings that begin something but do not end it, or have few imitators. The reason for this is that, unlike England, where periods and styles can generally be categorized and labelled with ease and confidence, one cannot take anything one sees in Scotland for granted. The idea of something approximating to Tudor followed by Jacobean, Carolean, Queen Anne and Georgian just simply cannot be followed. Ideas flowed in at different times and from different places, often out of date, and were adapted as and when those who picked them up had the occasion. Practically the only time when this was not the case was during the two hundred years or so that followed the arrival of Queen Margaret and the Normans in the eleventh century, when a settled, ordered society existed right up to the advent of Edward I and his foolish aggressions. Afterwards the effects of foreign treaties and deliberately not being English had a stultifying effect, which began to dissolve and become something progressive and recognizable again in the sixteenth century, only to be interfered with by the Reformation, when the blight of Calvinism all but prevented further progress and once more resulted in a further crop of individual and divergent efforts. That is one reason why one finds so many unique things north of the border.

Farnell is on an old site. Indeed, Lord Kinnaird, who is a keen historian and archaeologist, thinks Edward I himself may have built something there, though that does not necessarily follow, as the cathedral at Brechin is of Pictish origin and there could easily have been an episcopal manor on the site long before the thirteenth century. In any event, there is a little old bit at ground-floor level with battlements which may or may not have military origins. More pertinently, the Gothic gablets at the east end, replacing the more common crow-steps, are in the Flemish manner and certainly confirm their episcopal purpose, as does the crowned 'M', for the Virgin Mary, and 'Jesus-Maria' that are carved on opposite skew putts (corbelled ends to the gables).

The little palas-manor is entered by a semi-circular stair-tower topped with an ordinary projecting crow-stepped gable, the latter suggesting the late sixteenth century when, on the ejection of the bishops, the building was secularized. It has since been harled toothpaste pink, much to the disappointment of Lord Southesk, who, when I sent him a copy of the sketch that appears in these pages, said that, alas, it was not as posterity would now see it, he only wished it was. The sketch shows Farnell before its transformation, rendered necessary, at least the harling, by excessive zeal rather than the reverse. The walls became unsafe and had to be strengthened with concrete once the Victorian floors and fittings had been removed. It is often the case that this happens in old buildings. They tend to hold together until something is taken away, and then collapse or are radically weakened. This nearly happened at Druminnor when the later additions were taken down and the foundations exposed to unaccustomed pressure.

2. From Norman Keep
to Tower House

The unoccupied Place of Mochrum in Galloway was restored by the third Marquis of Bute as early as 1876. Had it not needed restoration, it would certainly have qualified as the oldest secular baronial house in Scotland in continuous habitation. The Marquis was the first of that noble family to show such a rare interest in art and architecture and to care as much for posterity as honour. His work at Cardiff Castle and Mount Stuart is well known, but throughout the length and breadth of the land he and his immediate successors have been busy resuscitating historic and beautiful buildings, both religious and secular, on a scale scarcely known previously. It is true that commerce and industry paid for this, but what a splendid use of profits. It is not what they are spent on today.

Mochrum is probably the oldest stone building of its kind, other than Drum, that has survived to such an extent. I say probably because, as we know, Traquair has claims that cannot be denied. It has certainly been inhabited most of its life and never restored or altered, apart from a recent re-harling and touch-up of the paintwork, since the end of the seventeenth century, but when its first stone tower was erected is unknown, and none of the recognizable authorities give any date for its commencement. One must, therefore, assume that the first building was of wood and that the oldest part of Traquair is the northern tower, which no doubt dates from the second half of the fifteenth century, when the ancestors of the present family acquired it after it had served for centuries as a royal hunting lodge. Mochrum, on the other hand, may date part of its northern stone tower to the reign of David II—that is, the mid-fourteenth century—when that monarch, Bruce's son, granted the barony to Patrick, Earl of March, of the Dunbar family. Another tower is fifteenth and sixteenth century.

The Dunbars remained in possession of Mochrum until

The Place of Mochrum, Wigtonshire

Victorian times and the acquisition, by inheritance, and restoration undertaken by the Marquis of Bute, which is a good record and symptomatic of Galloway's position on the geographical and political sidelines, away from the English Border and far from Edinburgh and the rest of Scotland. There had been an earlier fortress even here, almost certainly of wood, on an islet in the midst of this marshy, deserted land, similarly at Lochnaw, also in Galloway but nearer the coast. There the Agnews, Normans like the earls of March, were royal servants and may have been permitted to erect a stone tower on the king's behalf about 1423, which is perhaps earlier than the *turris et fortalicis* recorded as having existed at Traquair, when the present barons arrived, and not as old as the tower at Mochrum.

There are certain features peculiar to both Mochrum and Galloway which have been preserved and emphasized in Lord Bute's restoration, the most obvious being the form of the crow-steps, which in the case of the fourteenth-century entrance tower are blocky and strong, each made of a single piece of masonry, while in the younger tower each step is formed of several small stones and topped by an individual coping, a purely domestic feature seen only in the south-west. There is, of course, no harling anywhere, and practically the only addition, and not a restoration, is the small linking hall between the two towers. The latter were formerly quite separate and were built so; only a single

Huntingtower, formerly Gowrie Castle, Perthshire

wall joined them and protected the small courtyard behind. There are a number of Scottish houses and castles which grew in this strange way, with two or more towers standing in virtual isolation but which were eventually joined and made into one house. Traquair itself is an important one, following fairly closely on Huntingtower, in Perthshire, which is often quoted as the classic example. Here the process began with two separate towers, one L-shaped, the other rectangular, with a gap of some nine feet between them which remained unbridged until, it is said, an eloping daughter leapt across, shaking the household into roofing the chasm over.

Mochrum, almost lost in the midst of its wild and remote Machers, (moors), set with bogs and silent but for the birds and the beasts, has no history in the usual sense, no records of sieges or family tussles, whereas Huntingtower is all history—it has not even got its original name any more. It used to be the House of Ruthven and was the seat of the earls of Gowrie until one of them kidnapped the young James VI and through him ruled the country. James was no fool: he had been torn from his mother as a child, brought up by her detractors and surrounded by her enemies, so he knew just what to do when he reached an age and got the chance to do it. He escaped from Ruthven on the pretence of going hunting and got his own back in a dramatic and unexpected way. He made his own plot, lured the Gowries into a house in Perth and had them all arrested and many of them killed. The name and all memory of the original Ruthven were obliterated, the house called Huntingtower, somewhat appropriately, and the barony sequestrated by the Crown. The wording of the Act of Parliament in question states that it is 'ordained the baronie and place of Ruthven be changeit and callit in all tyme coming the place and baronie an Huntingtower'.

In 1643 the barony was given by Charles I to William Murray, son of the minister of Dysart, in Fife, and former 'whipping-boy' to the King when Duke of York. From him Huntingtower descended to the Murray dukes of Atholl until the end of the eighteenth century, when, after acting as a dower house, it became a calico factory. It is now in the care of the Department of the Environment, is roofed and whole and contains some of the finest and reputedly the earliest painted ceilings in Scotland. Besides the more normal geometrical patterns there are also figures, nude and otherwise, animals and birds, exotic foliage and heraldic creatures. Some of this resembles designs found in the valley of the Loire, in tapestries in particular, and dates from the first half of the sixteenth century, the oldest tower in the house itself being built a hundred years earlier. All of which brings us back to Traquair for very similar decorative features have been found there, the same dogs and pseudo-Renaissance features, for instance, under more modern plaster and panelling. Indeed, the present laird, the twentieth, was posed a problem by some painted beams he uncovered at one end of the high drawing-room, which, like most of the inhabitable interior, is in seventeenth-century Restoration style, painted and carved pine-wood. He decided, wisely probably, since this part of the house is regularly shown to visitors and hardly private any longer, to leave the beams exposed although they were of quite a different period.

Until Peter Maxwell Stuart came into his own here, Traquair

was a very secret sort of place, seemingly lost in the depths of the Peeblesshire countryside, set at the end of an overgrown avenue lined with centuries-old trees, a bit cobwebby, if one can use such a term, and altogether antique and charming in the dictionary sense of the word—that is, magical, with a touch of witchcraft,

Traquair House, Peeblesshire

though no witches are recorded there; almost as in a fairy story by Charles Perrault, *La Belle au bois dormant* perhaps. In fact, Traquair had not been altered in any noticeable way since the seventeenth century and was full of souvenirs of past ages, unmodernized and so decayingly beautiful that it had no rival in Scotland and none south of the Border.

Traquair is still full of remarkable souvenirs, including the bed in which Mary, Queen of Scots, slept her last, or it may have been her penultimate, night in Scotland before being rowed over the Solway to throw herself on the mercy of her cousin Elizabeth Tudor. The bed came from Terregles House, in Dumfriesshire, together with other things belonging to the Maxwell Stuart family when they inherited Traquair on the demise of Lady Louisa Stuart in 1878, she being the last of the old line and sister of the last Earl of Traquair. They were descended from the High Stewards of Scotland through a half-brother of James III of Scots and became lairds of Traquair in the late fifteenth century. Before that the barony had been either royally held or in the hands of royal nominees.

The building, which is very much a house and not a castle, though I have seen it called such, belongs to three periods. The first is in the form of a border tower, with a slight nib at one end to contain the staircase. This may have ancient foundations going back to the days when Traquair was a favourite haunt of the Stuart kings, but, as we shall see, most border towers began life as timber erections and all those so-called pele-towers, named after the wooden palisades that defended them, sprang up in their present form only from the mid-fifteenth century, when the first part of Traquair was built. This extended to about the middle of the existing main façade, the small stair projection being incorporated in the next extension and being provided with a conically capped turret as today. This was done in the early seventeenth century and was followed by the projecting of two high-roofed, single-storeyed wings and the enclosing of the front court within a magnificent wrought iron grille and gates. These are almost certainly the finest examples extant, or at any rate in original *situ* in Scotland. Their like once graced the entrance to Caroline Park, near Edinburgh, country seat of a contemporary Earl of Cromartie, but these have twice since been moved, first to a house outside Stirling and now to Gogar House, on the main road from Edinburgh to Glasgow, on the way to the airport. I mention them because so few people notice them as they rush to and fro, and they can so easily be seen without even getting out of one's car.

More famous than these handsome Caroline gates at Traquair are the 'steekit', or stuck, gates at the end of the grassy avenue and about which a number of legends exist. The best known records how the then Earl of Traquair, after receiving Prince Charles Edward, swore never to open his gates again until a Stuart was restored to the throne. The main argument against this is that the gates in question, including their posts topped with heraldic bears, were not put up until some years later. Another theory is that on the death of the last 'Coontess' the Earl declared he would open them only for another, which there never was. Probably both stories are wrong since the gates appear to have no hinges and were very likely never intended to be opened. They are something much more interesting, namely a magnificent folly.

Of course, the idea of a long grassy avenue through the trees to the *manoir*, or *château*, is quite common in France, and there is nothing so French in Scotland as Traquair. The subject of French-

Detail of wrought ironwork, Traquair House, with Earl's coat of arms.

ness is Scottish culture has long been debated and queried, some denying its significance, others overstating it. What one can say is that in royal palaces and the homes of the greater magnates direct French influence can be see. At Huntly Castle, in Aberdeenshire, for instance, the uppermost storey, with its row of oriel windows, clearly reflects the northern side of Blois, but the Marquis of Huntly in the seventeenth century was married to a French-woman and lived for a time in exile at Blois. Then there is the François I staircase at Fyvie, which was the creation of Alexander Seton, Lord Fyvie, and later Earl of Dunfermline, who became Chancellor of Scotland and guardian of the royal children and was a much travelled and erudite man. That French craftsmen were employed at Holyrood and Falkland Palaces, as well as at Linlithgow and Stirling, goes without saying, but all this was outwith the experience of the ordinary laird and feudal baron, and any observable French influence in their houses was certainly secondhand and often not really French at all.

Having said this, Traquair certainly does look French, and is the most authentically French-looking building in Scotland, not for its few romantic turrets, nor for its fairy castle aspect, both of

Renaissance staircase at Fyvie Castle, Aberdeenshire, in the style of François I

which are seen to a much greater degree in Scottish castles of the late sixteenth and early seventeenth centuries in Aberdeenshire, but for its setting at the end of its lovely avenue, its tall, domestic roofs of a kind virtually unknown in England, and above all its weathered maturity. This is not often so obvious, with people forever tidying up their properties, painting them, altering them, thinking they are improving them and generally taking from them all that historic and architectural character that gives them their charm. Old things, like old people, should be allowed to show their age, gracefully and in peace. They should never be over-restored but instead renovated, and only those things done which are absolutely necessary. The re-harling of Traquair had to be done, and it had been done sensitively, not in glaring 'snow-cem' but in a neutral shade that matches rather than contrasts with the stonework. This re-harling, a certain amount of plumbing and paintwork, plus a little re-arrangement of the internal planning so that the laird can live more modestly in his house and show as much of it as possible to the public, is practically all that has happened to Traquair in three hundred years.

Traquair has been likened to the Manoir de Courtangis, in the Perche district of Normandy, just north of the valley of the Loire, and that is certainly where I would place it if I did not know and came upon it suddenly from nowhere. It is not exactly like Courtangis, which has a central stair turret and other arrangements not the same, but in the same sort of wooded setting, with tall roofs and small but decidedly non-martial turrets, attracting one from a discreet distance. Yet despite this its growth has been natural and not consciously copied from anything in particular, and that, perhaps, is part of its uniqueness, our not being able to classify it. It is certainly the only border tower to my knowledge that has evolved as it has—that is, sideways in preference to upwards—and become neither castle nor mansion but a true *manoir*.

In his guide to the house the laird mentions the Borderland bristling with pele towers and suggests that these were built to repel the English at the time of the War of Independence, but even if Traquair itself was in existence, in stone, at the time, few others were. As we have seen, stone towers other than royal did not become common sights until the mid-fifteenth century, and most were erected later. They began life as tiny imitations of

Norman keeps, square and rude, built in the Borders not just to repel English reivers (raiders) but any raiders. A typical border keep of the fifteenth century had a vaulted lower floor into which stolen cattle were driven, or from which one's own were removed, one room over another, and timber floors linked only by a spiral staircase within the thickness of the walls. At the top was a bartisan (lookout) and possibly castellations, though these were not common until the sixteenth century and even then not universal; the tower would have stood within a timber stockade.

It is, perhaps, in the evolution of these towers, which became what have been properly termed 'tower houses', that a genuine Scottish style can be seen to have developed which has no counterpart anywhere else and which, in contrast to the more sporadic outbursts of other styles in the north, was continuous in its growth. In due course the primitive square keeps that bristled over the Borders acquired that small nib that took the stairs separately, as at Traquair, and this nib eventually turned into a complete arm, making the plan no longer rectangular but L-shaped, with the stair turret being at the re-entrant angle as it was called. Subsequently various other refinements appeared, principally with the discovery of gunpowder, the most curious of which was the Z-plan, consisting of a rectangular main hall with round towers at each end set diagonally so that attackers could be fired on from behind, so to speak.

Here we are getting onto the subject of castles *per se* which I have dealt with at length in another book. One might mention, however, so that readers can more easily grasp what I mean, that the largest Z-shaped castle in Scotland is also the best known, namely Glamis. Of L-shaped examples there are scores; it is the most common plan in the whole country and refers not only to castles and manor houses but to farms and houses in streets; many of our older towns can boast a tall L-shaped mansion, sometimes quite modest in size, with crow-stepped gables, turret and wheel-stair in the re-entrant angle. That they descend from Norman keeps would surprise some of their occupants, but it is so, and this evolution continued, in its Scottish domestic form, well into the seventeenth century, when all need for defence or martial appearance had become unnecessary and mere affectation.

The evolution of these tower houses, which are the commonest form of manor house or baronial seat in Scotland, is worth exploring for a while, since, apart from the initial nib adjunct for the stairs, and the L-shape, it had other interesting variations. Almost invariably these variations were associated with a growth in height rather than length and in the end with the topmost

Branxholm Tower, near Hawick, a Scott seat

storeys becoming the most important and decorative. This idea reached its apotheosis in the castles of mid-Aberdeenshire, Crathes (actually Kincardineshire), Craigievar and Fraser, which are no more castles in the defensive sense than a long, low manor house is, only their creators were following what had become the native tradition in architecture, a tradition that only slowly changed and took on more cosmopolitan aspects as the seventeenth century progressed and the effect of the Union of the Crowns became more widespread.

One small wall survives in the kitchen of an existing farmhouse near Hawick of Fenwick Tower, not enough to show what the building was like, but not far away is the more concrete example of Branxholm. This was the ancient seat of the Scotts of Buccleuch and, although much restored and added to, it still sits nicely across the valley from Fenwick, gay with its baronial banner

Darnick Tower, Melrose

unfurled to greet the passer-by. It was once a simple tower and could scarcely ever have housed either the twenty-nine knights or their banners that Sir Walter Scott mentions in the *Lay of the Last Minstrel*, but then the Bard of Abbotsford was more interested in the spirit of things, which he surely got splendidly, than in precise historical fact. The tower he loved the best was Darnick, near Melrose, so much so that he became known to his friends as 'the Duke of Darnick'. It is diminutive and certainly keep-like, with castellations, crow-steps, stone roof and projecting stair turret, the latter, however, not so much at one end of the square but assymetrically placed, which is rare. This tiny 'toy castle' dates from the sixteenth century with later improvements and is still occupied, having a feudal baroness as its châtelaine.

Scott's sense of atmosphere and of the heroic spirit is difficult to condemn, though occasionally one must criticize even him whose own spirit embodies that of the Borders as a whole and did

Priest's hole, Traquair

so much to show the remarkable homogeneity of the Scottish people and to bring them closer together with their ex-enemies south of the Border. Amongst his more conjectural stories is the one by which the hunted Montrose, seeking refuge with the Earl of Traquair after the Battle of Philiphaugh, knocked at the door only to find the Earl 'not at home'. It is not a nice story and may in part have been invented, but not how the 'trimmer' Earl, ostensibly a 'King's man', espied Montrose coming and hid himself in an upstairs room, ignored the pleas for help and did not come down until the coast was clear. The celebrated door-knocker, which Scott so admired and imagined had felt the hand of the

Amisfield Tower, Dumfriesshire

greatest Scottish hero since Bruce, was not there in Montrose's day but dates from the 1690s. Scott was right, however, in his story of Gilbert Broun, the Abbot of Sweetheart, who was preserved in his position long after the Reformation largely through the intervention of the Maxwells of Terregles, who themselves are still Roman Catholics and even preserve at Traquair a priest's hole. These are more common in England, and in Scotland are associated with the Jacobite rather than earlier periods. There is still, too, at Traquair a Roman Catholic chapel in one of the side-wings, containing finely carved wooden panels thought to have come from Mary of Guise's chapel in Leith.

Dumfriesshire, whence so many famous Scottish families emigrated northwards, not just the Maxwells and Stuarts but the Bruces and Douglasses, Irvines and even Gordons, was known as 'the debateable land' because it was never wholly English or Scots and in theory at least was controlled by a condominium. It is there that some of the best-preserved tower houses have survived—indeed, the best, which is at Amisfield and deserves to stand with the most celebrated Aberdeenshire castles as a supreme example of the fully developed Scottish style.

Today Amisfield, the old tower of the Charteris family, whose arms can still be seen on its walls, stands roofed and hale, thought not inhabitable, in the grounds of a later Georgian house, well guarded and maintained by its owners. It counts seven storeys, the topmost forming a room five feet by six which rides the roof ridge of the sixth like someone on a hobbyhorse. It gives access to the firebucket-cum-chimney which would have been lit in time of raid. This one surely was never lit, the tower being built in the early seventeenth century, after such lawlessness had ceased. Yet there are numerous shot-holes from which an imaginary enemy could be potshotted at, and almost all the interesting parts of the building are on the top three storeys, well out of harm's way at the base. The ground floor only is vaulted, with a straight stair up to the first floor, whence a spiral ascends at one corner to the third floor, itself linked with the topmost floors by further smaller spirals. There are three double-storeyed corner turrets, conically capped, and very sophisticated dormers made in the form of imitation *bretêches*—that is, with holes, false in this case, which in an original would have been used for pouring boiling lead or other deterrents down upon intruders. In almost every respect, including date, Amisfield Tower displays the characteristics of larger, better-known edifices in Aberdeenshire, yet it has no direct links with any of them.

Amisfield used to possess a fine carved oak door in the Renaissance manner showing Samson and the lion. A similarly designed and executed example was taken from Terregles to

Traquair depicting the lion fighting with the unicorn; it can be seen just at the foot of the spiral stair there.

Such carvings and the generally high standard of workmanship found in such places in Jacobean and Carolean times discount the notion that folk then lived in uncomfortable,

Scotstarvit Tower, Fife

somewhat crude surroundings. Besides decent woodwork, painted beams and handsome chimneypieces, they had wall hangings and rugs, cushioned windowseats and respectable furniture. They were also, on the whole, better educated than many of us today. A recent commentary made on the quarter-centenary of a well-known university college, not at Oxford, suggested that the thing Jacobean graduates would notice if they were to come back today would not be so much our greater comfort, technical achievements or agnosticism but our lack of culture. They did not dress or behave like barbarians, they could write and read several languages, even in the antique, and they knew more in proportion about their world than many students now, though there are today more students and more subjects to study. One has only to think of the young Montrose, who, in his teens, having already produced an heir to the Carnegies, was sent abroad to learn fencing at Angers, manners and music in Paris, or the youthful John Clerk of Penicuik, who, studying law at Leyden, made his way over the Alps to Italy, acquired tastes far in excess of his pocket and returned home via France, having invented a species of 'Grand Tour' long before it became general in the eighteenth century.

More pertinent, perhaps, to the present narrative was the life in a tower such as Scotstarvit, in Fife, which with Amisfield in Dumfriesshire and Coxton in Morayshire forms a trio of almost perfectly preserved seventeenth-century tower houses, each with its own peculiar evolution from the original Norman keep. Scotstarvit dates from the early part of the century in which the Union of the Crowns took place and yet is a building that could have been put up two hundred years earlier. Square, but for the necessary nib to contain the stairs, it is completely plain until parapet level is reached, when the stair nib is topped with a conical stone turret. There is also a small doocot (pigeon-cote) at roof level and three chimneystalks, one of which comes straight up at the parapet, not at the gable end, and is held in position by a flying buttress. Inside are two vaulted ceilings, each with an intermediate floor in timber, and above is the laird's private room with fine Renaissance chimneypiece. Here Sir John Scot of Scotstarvit, the Scottish Montaigne, wrote his *Staggering state of Scots Statesmen*, and Blaeu's atlas was projected. Here too were assembled the poets and thinkers of Carolean Scotland. Sir John's wife was the sister of Drummond of Hawthornden, whose poems were of such a calibre that Ben Jonson trudged all the way up from London to Midlothian to congratulate their author in person. Another contemporary was Sir Thomas Urquhart of Cromarty, who was the first to translate Rabelais into English. So to think of the inmates of these tower houses as primitive or ignorant would certainly be a mistake.

Coxton dates from as late as 1644, yet reverts to the earliest type of 'keep-tower' with castellated battlement at one corner, stone roof and stairs carried up within the thickness of the walls. It was entered at first-floor level, the basement being for animals and storage, and each floor is stone vaulted, but in opposite directions in order to give added strength. It is, in fact, built entirely of stone and was the *caput* of the barony of the Inneses of Invermarkie. Its only known occupants seem to have been farmhands and a

Coxton Tower, Moray

gardener, yet it is contemporary in time, but not in architectural characteristics, with Innes House. This latter is a mansion on the L-plan in which almost all the details are imported from the south and where the stairs are scale-and-platt—straight up and down with landing, not spiral, and the parapet ornamental, not battlemented.

The three towers, Amisfield, Scotstarvit and Coxton are in date and style reversed. That is to say, Amisfield, the oldest, is the most modern, Coxton the least so, and although all three are 'fortified', none saw any kind of warfare, civil or otherwise. They sum up in themselves almost the whole development of the Scottish tradition in building as it evolved from the 'peel-cum-keep' of the Middle Ages into the domestic tower house. Almost, because there is a fourth style which I have not so far mentioned. This consisted of building onto the very top of the older towers a

Preston Tower, East Lothian: note doocot

sort of penthouse, and the lairds and barons living up there in eyries. Hence Charles II's reputed remark on being entertained in Dreel Castle, in Fife: 'What a good dinner I've gotten in a crow's nest.'

The two prime examples of this penthouse style are Spedlins, in Dumfriesshire, and Preston, in Midlothian. In the first case a rectangular Norman keep, with walls ten feet thick, was topped by an extra two storeys and attic in the seventeenth century with average wall thickness of three feet. This addition had corner turrets with decorated mouldings around the corbelling, pedimented windows of classical inspiration and a magnificent Renaissance chimneypiece. The new abode must have been difficult of access, however, with only spirals and other stairs within the thickness of the lower walls, and was built on top of two vaulted chambers, the bottom-most of which was a dungeon. In it the baron is said to have put a local miller, without

Spedlin's Tower, Dumfriesshire

Lord Magdalen's House, Prestonpans

intent to leave him there, but went off to Edinburgh and forgot, and the poor man died. The present laird says this is not true, though local tradition will have it so. It also suggests that that is why the lower portion of the building was allowed to fill up with rubble and dirt so as to obliterate all recollection of the event. Certainly the place has a depressing air about it, despite the red stone of which it is built and the pleasant countryside round about. Spedlins is being restored.

Preston Tower, in Midlothian, not far from the site of the Battle of Prestonpans, in which Prince Charlie's forces routed the forces of George II in just ten minutes, is less depressing to took at but more dramatic. Here is another square tower with completely Renaissance top, two storeys in which the Hamilton baron of the place installed himself towards the end of the sixteenth century. He does not seem to have been too happy up there and early in the seventeenth century came down, building himself a pleasant two-storeyed mansion in the street below, with no suggestions of martial history or taste; it is nicely crow-stepped and faces three sides of a courtyard, with corner turret on one side and attractive projecting entry, and replete with baronial heraldry on the other. The house is called Magdalen's, after the Hamilton Law Lord of that name, and is occupied, having been restored by the late Robert Hurd on behalf of the National Trust for Scotland.

Curiously enough, almost immediately opposite is Northfield

Northfield House, Prestonpans

House, the home of Lord Magdalen's brother-in-law, which is tall and picturesque in the more old-fashioned tower-house style, as it arrived in its final development, with amusing corner turrets, or 'studies', high-pitched roof and dormers. The entrance, on the other hand, shows an attempt at being classical, and inside are some of Scotland's best painted ceilings, the flower and vegetable variety as well as the animal kind, as at Traquair and Huntingtower, though these cannot possibly be so old, as the building dates from 1611. It is the home of Mr Schomberg Scott, formerly architectural adviser to the National Trust, and has been nicely renovated by him—the term is his own. There was a doocot pertaining to Northfield, which can still be seen but is no longer on the property, and another double one of the kind

called 'lectern', on account of its sloping shape, beside the old Preston Tower.

Northfield developed on the lines of Traquair—that is to say, it lengthened itself. It could, probably, not have gone upwards any more, but of course it does not have Traquair's antiquity or appearance of seigneurial grace and age. Fountainhall, on the other hand, does and is one of the few reasonably sized manor houses that can be compared with it.

Sitting pleasantly on an East Lothian hillside between Haddington and Pencaitland, spoilt only by unnecessarily large electric pylons that march over the fields in a most aggressive manner, Fountainhall began life as an L-shaped house but was first extended along the L and then had a brand-new wing added at right angles to the main building. Features of the place include, besides an attractive mellowness achieved by the proprietors leaving something to the imagination and not tidying everything up, a sundial high up on the south-western corner of the older building, and two spiral stairs, one corbelled out in the re-entrant angle with turret above, and another on the north front within a semi-circular projection that reaches to the ground, a less normal arrangement in Scotland. The upper floor of the later, Carolean addition is reached via an external, canopied stair. It comprises one large room, or hall, and was used as a minor court of law by Sir John Lauder, whose legal title was Lord Fountainhall. This may or may not represent a latter-day continuing of the older baronial form of justice practised in Norman times—probably not, though the jougs (neck braces) used to tie up miscreants awaiting sentence were said to have been hanging near the door! It is perhaps worth mentioning that long galleries, of which this may be considered a sort but known as the ballroom, were not so common a feature in Scotland as in England and became fashionable only later in seventeenth century. This was for obvious reasons: tall tower houses and turreted castles hardly lent themselves to such expansiveness, though at Crathes there is a rare example, ceiled in oak, and formerly part chapel and part baron's court.

Most baronial houses and small castles of the sixteenth and even seventeenth centuries in Scotland were surrounded by a

Fountainhall, East Lothian

high wall, called a barmkin; in the case of castles this was punctuated with towers and other features, a good specimen being at Craigievar, where one old round tower, high-roofed like a witch's hat and older than the castle itself, remains on the west side of the drive. These walls evolved from the wooden stockades

Ardblair, Perthshire

and palisades which enclosed the pele towers and keeps in the Borders, and also from the larger castles of *enceinte*—that is, castles in which the keep was superseded by a fortified gatehouse and enclosing wall, the rest of the buildings, hall, stables, brewhouse and chapel being attached to the wall at various points. In the seventeenth century such walls were retained as garden and courtyard enclosures but were still fairly sturdy. Fountainhall shows this well, the garden keeping its original outer walls and seventeenth-century gateway. There are as well two fine lectern doocots, one with holes for doves, the other only a shed, built in replica to produce symmetry, which was important at the time.

The courtyard plan, as it was called, became a style on its own and, although more applicable to royal palaces and larger buildings generally, had its imitators amongst the less grand manors and castles. Of these none better displays it than Ardblair, in Perthshire, which is built entirely around and within walls yet dates from the seventeenth and later centuries and is wholly domestic and private in character.

Ardblair is the home of the Oliphants of Gask, a branch of that well-known Jacobite family which entertained Bonnie Prince Charlie in 1745 and one of whom was the celebrated Lady Nairne, author of so many lovely Scottish songs and the setter to music of the best of Burns. Her piano is treasured in the house, together with many Jacobite souvenirs, including a fine portrait of the Prince, before which a white rose is always placed, his gloves, Order of the Garter and white-cockaded bonnet. An ancestor of the present baron of Blair was aide-de-camp to Prince Charlie and had to flee to the Continent after Culloden. The family stayed abroad for nearly twenty years and then assembled these precious relics. Gask, where the Prince had breakfasted, was demolished and a newer, Regency-style house erected in its stead, not at all to the taste of the author of 'Will ye no come back again', whose watercolour of the 'Auld Hoose o' Gask' hangs in her room at Ardblair. Both the Oliphant and Blair families are of Norman origin, one of the Blairs being knighted by Alexander III and made Steward of Fife.

Amongst the many fine portraits at Ardblair is the rather surprising and somewhat theatrical one of James Gillespie, architect of much of Edinburgh's Georgian New Town and one of the competitors for the rebuilt Houses of Parliament at Westminster, his sketch for which is also in the house. James Gillespie married into the Graham family, which was connected with the Oliphants, and thus he acquired enhanced social status, an enhancement he made considerable use of in his work, by adding Graham to his name and becoming known to posterity as Gillespie Graham.

Ardblair is a quaint house which, beginning at one corner with the nucleus of an L-shaped tower, runs round three sides, the fourth being enclosed by a high wall and semi-circular entrance gateway. The small courtyard beyond is delightful and contains a fine many-faceted sundial.

Also in Perthshire is Stobhall, another courtyard structure and another house closely associated with the Forty-five. It was a dower house of the Drummonds, the first of whom came to

Scotland with Queen Margaret in the eleventh century. He is said to have navigated the ship that brought her north, and the wavy lines on the Drummond coat of arms represent the waves of the sea.

Stobhall, or Stobschaw as it is sometimes called, stands on a

Interior of the chapel, Stobhall, Perthshire

wooded bluff overlooking the River Tay just north of Perth, is entered through a gatehouse and, although seeming all-of-a-piece, is in reality of several periods. The house proper dates only from the eighteenth century, when it became the home of the Drummond ladies, who, not suffering the same disabilities as their Jacobite menfolk, were allowed to stay in Scotland. The first Duke of Perth, made so by James VII and II after he had become a Roman Catholic, had to go into exile with his master, and for more than a century his successors, despite the occasional appearance in Scotland in support of the rebellions of 1715 and 1745, were obliged to live abroad until Queen Victoria withdrew their attainder. They did not, however, formally return to part of their historic inheritance until more recently, when Stobhall, originally listed as in the care of Ancient Monuments, was made over to the present Earl, not Duke, of Perth, and his family. They have made this modest manor most attractive and, indeed, the Earl has been active as a Crown Estate Commissioner.

The Jacobean garden with its interesting sundial and yew trees have survived and the chapel and priest's house have been restored. These latter are the oldest parts of Stobhall, the priest's house having housed the Ruskins and Millaises during a wife-swapping episode. The chapel contains one of the finest painted

Maxwelton House, Dumfriesshire

ceilings in the country, and the best preserved. It is devoted to the armorial devices and simplified portraits of Charles I and contemporary sovereigns, plus Prester John and other more legendary figures. The colours are bright and clear, the ceiling having been partially repainted in the nineteenth century, though not badly. The original stone *mensa* (altar) has been re-erected and furnished, and at one side is a traditional Scottish aumbry (cupboard) with pierced and decorated door to allow air into the place where the sacred vessels were kept. There is good stained glass in the windows, and the floor has been covered with rush matting.

Chapels are something of a feature of Scottish houses, some Roman Catholic, others Episcopalian, but unlike their English counterparts most of them are actually in separate buildings not in the house itself. A slightly more modern example is at Maxwelton, in Dumfriesshire, and belongs to the last days of the direct line of the Lauries of that Ilk. At that time the inheritance went to a former rector of St George's Church, Bloomsbury, who not only enjoyed officiating in the chapel but trained young curates there and housed them on the estate. The Lauries came to Maxwelton in the early seventeenth century. Before that it had been the property of the Cunninghames, as represented by the earls of Glencairn, and had passed under the name of Glencairn Castle. The precise wording of the deed of purchase describes the place as 'Castle, Tower, Fortalice and Manorplace of Glencairn'. By then it had already lost all pretence of being a real castle and had become a typical Jacobean tower house, the core of which can still be made out in the larger building that presently covers the site; in fact, it came more to light recently when the Stenhouses, who acquired it in 1968, began their demolishing, rebuilding and restoring of the place.

Already, before they left, the Lauries had obtained permission to demolish two-thirds of Maxwelton House, and the new owners mercifully reduced this to such extraneous and unhistorical quarters as the ballroom, and re-creating from amongst the cleared Victorian excrescences a house in the Scottish vernacular, with courtyard, crow-steps, wheel-stair in the re-entrant angle, dormers and semi-circular arched entry, plus a new swimming-pool in the same traditional style! It is all a bit like a Scottish version of a Spanish *parador*, but beautifully done. The stonework is superb and shows how the craftsmanship necessary to achieve this has not entirely died out and that private patronage still has a role to play.

Maxwelton used to straggle and was far too big, and only part of it was of architectural or historic interest. It did, however, have a pleasant pink appearance, with a couple of old bay windows that somehow spoke of the period when Admiral Laurie lived there. These have gone, though surviving internally, while the Stenhouses unearthed a little vaulted room which is said to be associated with the heroine of the world-renowned ballad 'Maxwelton Braes are bonny': the Annie, or rather Anna, Laurie for whom William Douglas of Fingland swore he would lay down his head and die. She was the daughter of Robert Laurie and Jean Riddell, whose coat of arms graces the space above the door at the foot of the wheel-stair, and she turned down the Jacobite Douglas

The arms of Anna Laurie's parents, Maxwelton House

Craigdarroch House, married home of Anna Laurie

for the safer, staunchly Hanoverian Alexander Fergusson of Craigdarroch.

The Riddells, Lauries and Fergussons were the three principal lairds in the district and in Burns' time took part in the episode he immortalized, if that is the right word, in 'The Whistle'. This referred to an ebony whistle which would belong to whoever was sober enough to be able to blow it after a night of conviviality. The Fergusson of the time, Anna Laurie's son, won the bout, and to this day the whistle remains at Craigdarroch, though that fine Adam house is no longer a Fergusson manor. Like Maxwelton it has older foundations, but today it is a pink and white confection of the utmost charm, seeming more rococo in feeling than the usual Baroque beloved of its often heavy-handed architect, recalling more the powder-pink and amusing curly-whirlies of a South German church, the monastery of Einselden, than a Gallovidian mansion. The Fergussons were amongst the oldest of local families in a region where such things still matter and obtained their original barony from Robert Bruce himself.

Maxwelton's rejuvenation won a Saltire Award, which is given annually for new or restored Scottish houses, but it could not have been done without ample private funds. Another private restoration was the House of Aldie, on the borders of Fife and Perthshire. I described this fully in my book on Scottish castles but I think it worth mentioning again briefly on two accounts: its restitution was the boyhood dream of a Scot working abroad, a dream fulfilled in retirement, and since his demise the glaring white with which the architect had enveloped it has been toned down to a pleasant grey that matches the stonework. Some thirty to forty properties of this kind have been restored since the last war, though not all have been completed, and most have been the subject of Historic Buildings Council grants. Would-be restorers seem to start off with enthusiasm but often flag when the money runs out or the strings attached become irksome. The first government grants were made in 1954, and amongst these funds were provided to repair the fabric of the priory at Pittenweem and to paint the exterior, to re-harl Traquair and also do some painting there, and for restoration of the ogee-roofed gazebos at Melville, which were used as master's 'digs' when the house was a school. At a later date a grant was made for the work at Druminnor but subsequently withdrawn when the restorers dispensed with the services of the late Dr Douglas Simpson, than whom no more able or sympathetic adviser could have been employed.

At Braikie, just inland from Arbroath, the farmer on whose land a delightful and comparatively well-preserved L-shaped manor house stands applied for a grant but withdrew when he found the amount offered insufficient to modernize the place, merely enough to make the building wind- and weatherproof. One would not suppose that public funds would run to more unless it included old panelling and interior decorations of an historic kind, which Braikie has not got, and, of course, when one does get a grant, the restored building must be open by request so that we can see where our money has gone!

Braikie is the perfect type of L-shaped tower of the Jacobean period, neither castle nor house but a little of both. Until recently it was fully roofed, and restoration would have been a much more viable proposition than today, though compared to some other examples it is still pretty hale. It was built by Thomas Fraser whose 'fraises', or heraldic strawberries appear on the coat of

Braikie, a Fraser manor in Angus

arms on the stair turret which is corbelled out over the entrance. This family was one of the many who made their way by degrees from France to the Borders and after Bannockburn were rewarded for their support of Robert Bruce with properties in central and northern Scotland. Their principal seat was at Muchall-in-Mar, since renamed Castle Fraser, where Andrew Fraser created what is in effect the first truly Scottish country house—that is, a towered and turreted mansion in the manner of French *châteaux* of substance, with defences turned into ornament, Renaissance parapets and decorative motifs, chapel and projecting outbuildings. All this in the reign of Charles I.

At Braikie things are much simpler, yet unique as well, for here, in this red sandstone tower roofed with sepia-hued Angus slates, are five bedrooms, two of them with *garderobes* (privies), a five-foot-wide wheel-stair that occupies the whole of the ground floor of the northern wing, and a baron's private room above. The latter is gained both by the smaller stairs in the re-entrant angle and by a 'secret' flight within the wall space. All this dates from 1582, with Amisfield, Scotstarvit and Coxton approximately twenty, thirty and fifty years later! They contain but one room above another and have absolutely no comparable comforts and planning arrangements. Braikie, however, has its defences, a great iron yett (gate) inside the door, wide shot-holes angled to take muskets at ground level, and iron bars over the larger windows. The holes under the upper windows are not shot-holes but shut-holes, so named for the little wooden slides inside which could be opened to allow air into the room, the windows being generally fixed.

A house which did have a grant, but one of a rather unusual kind, is Pourie, or Powrie, on a hill overlooking the advancing suburbs of Dundee. This splendid little manor, two storeyed and charming with its single round turret at one end, galleried entry on the first floor, swept dormers and attendant ancient 'keep' nearby, was saved from complete dereliction by the National Trust for Scotland, who bought it, then re-sold to a restoring purchaser. The place had been used as pigsties and all sorts of things, and it must have seemed pretty daunting to Peter Clarke and his wife when they first began their work of restitution. They had hoped to tackle the adjacent 'keep' as well in due course, but this was probably a little over-ambitious. The 'keep' dates from the latter half of the fifteenth century, the two-storeyed manor from the beginning of the seventeenth, and they were joined by other buildings and a barmkin wall around a courtyard. The standard of workmanship is very high both in the remains of the 'keep', which has a fine 'flat' arched and moulded doorway and a large 'flamboyant' chimneypiece, and in the restored part, which has two Renaissance windows and a refined plan in which two porches at first-floor level protect the laird's apartment at the western end, and the rest of the rooms.

Powrie was a Fotheringham seat whose dower house was at Murroes, a few miles to the east, set back from the coast road from Dundee to Arbroath in a pleasant glen and, somewhat unusually for Scotland, near a small hamlet and church, as one might expect in England. There is a doocot, but no longer on the property, which is inhabited—one might almost say suburbanized, since it was restored at a bad period and the grounds were reduced to a narrowish strip such as one might find in a row of houses and not a small manor. Like Powrie, Murroes is built of that madder-coloured stone which is so typical of the district and roofed in sepia Angus slates, really split stones, which acquire a lovely

Murroes, a Fotheringham manor near Dundee

yellow lichen that gives them a special character. It is two-storeyed only and possessed of a semi-circular, conically capped tower which, however, in this case is fairly unique in that instead of being corbelled out externally, just above the base as many Scottish stair towers are, it is corbelled out inside the house, rising outside directly from the ground. Murroes dates from the seventeenth century, is quite small and lacks obvious defensive features. Anyone wishing to live in a 'castle' could choose many much worse places and most of them a great deal larger; only the garden is a little restricting, if manageable.

Another attractive little manor house actually in a village, though without any garden or grounds at all, being at the cross-roads, right amongst the houses, is at Fordyce, in Banffshire. Some would say this is the most attractive of all the smaller 'houses of 'fens' (houses of defence) in the country. Certainly it boasts in miniature a large number of the features normally found in larger buildings, which perhaps accounts for its being known as 'the castle'. It was built for a provost of Aberdeen, one Thomas Menzies, in 1592, though the barony dates from much earlier,

Fordyce being associated with two more purely local families, the Ogilvies and the Abercrombies, whose tombs are in the ruins of their respective aisles in the nearby kirkyard, together with appropriate heraldic insignia.

The 'castle' at Fordyce is quite small and has had to be added to

The 'castle' at Fordyce, Banff

to become habitable in more modern times but in its original form was L-planned, with the usual spiral stair turret corbelled out in the re-entrant angle above the main, oak-studded door. The entry displays a veritable battery of shot-holes, below and above the first window, and the corbelling is very rich indeed. There are projecting turrets at two opposite corners and a date stone, but internally nothing of antiquity has survived, while the sash windows replace the older shutterboard variety, which were prevalent all over Scotland in the first half of the seventeenth century. These were formed with fixed leaded lights in the upper half and a wooden shutter below, which opened completely to the air. Fordyce has lain empty for some time but was lived in until quite recently and could easily be made habitable again. One hopes it will be, since the village itself has won a special award for its well-kept and pleasant appearance.

Not in the middle of a village but in a city, in the capital of

Scotland to be precise, is the manor of Coates. Sometimes called a hunting lodge, since it once stood in the midst of the Forest of Drumsheugh, of which a few trees still enclose it, this little turreted manor strikes an unusual note beside the towering mass of Sir George Gilbert Scott's St Mary's Cathedral. In fact, the

Easter Coates Manor, Edinburgh

cathedral was built with money gained from the sale of property in the neighbourhood and from Feu Duties from the surrounding late Georgian and early Victorian houses. Coates manor belonged at the end of the eighteenth century to the Walker family, of whom Sir Patrick Walker was Usher of the White Rod to the Crown of Scotland, in which capacity he attended the coronation of George IV and assisted in the fancy-dress pageantry of that monarch's progress through Edinburgh in 1822.

The last royal visitor to Scotland had been Bonnie Prince Charlie, who held brief court at Holyrood in 1745. Sir Walter Scott was mainly responsible for the success of 'heilan' Geordie's' trip north, when not only the King but the Lord Mayor of London appeared in the kilt, over silk tights. Scott had said that George IV was the first of his House that patriotic Scotsmen could accept, since he did not ascend the throne until after the death of the last of the Stuarts, Cardinal York, Prince Charles Edward's brother, in 1807. In the procession that went to Leith to greet George IV, Scott himself travelled by carriage with the Officers of State, but White Rod went on horseback, next to the Lord Lyon. He donned his crimson and gold coronation robes, and his horse was caparisoned in scarlet trimmed with white lace. Lyon wore his crown of office, a rarely seen object of crimson velvet with cincture of gold and strawberry leaf which James IV had once placed on a predecessor's head at a banquet at Holyrood. Such pageantry was not entirely inappropriate either, especially in the case of Sir Patrick Walker, for the manor of Coates, once part of the barony of Broughton, was royal and ecclesiastical in origin, having been created in 1128 by King David I, the veritable founder of Holyrood.

Sir Patrick Walker was a keen antiquarian and had already restored the manor of Coates, adding to its ornaments a number of carved stones and armorial features taken from buildings in the Old Town of Edinburgh, notably from the former French Ambassador's house in the High Street. Inside too, plaster moulds from the elaborately carved vaulting at Rosslyn Chapel were installed, similar to those Scott used at Abbotsford.

On Sir Patrick's death the manor went to his sisters Barbara and Mary, after whom the two west towers of St Mary's Cathedral are named and whose fortune paid for the erection of that building, the largest cathedral church erected in Britain since St Paul's, London, and the biggest in Scotland. Eventually the little manor house, not quite dwarfed but very nearly so by its huge neighbour, became first the house of the dean of Edinburgh and then the seat of the only *bona fide* choir school in Scotland recognized by Lord Lyon and by him granted a coat of arms. It is the modern equivalent of the old 'sang schules' of pre-Reformation days, and of the chapels royal at Stirling and Holyrood. As for the office of White Rod, it belongs to the Walker Trust, represented at the last coronation by the then bishop of Edinburgh.

3. Lairds' Houses

At a recent royal garden party at Holyroodhouse, a friend of mine
was greeted by a Highland acquaintance as an OFF. This completely mystified him and was also slightly embarrassing because
he was on duty as a Royal Archer and the Queen was just a few
yards away. It turned out that OFF means Old Fife Family, which
his is not, he coming from the West of Scotland, but there is
something in this Old Fife Family business, since Fife, often
called 'the Kingdom', since it once constituted a sub-kingdom of
Pictland, is very separate from the rest of the country, and Fifers
are a race on their own. The county, which is the only one in
Scotland to survive as an entity in the national regionalization
scheme, is very much a peninsula, facing the Lothians across the
'Scots Sea' to the south, and Angus over the Firth of Tay to the
north, and shut off on the west by sizeable hills. In the days,
when travel by water was easier and more common than by land,
Fife was occupied by Normans, in the baronies, and by Dutch
and Belgians who came over the North Sea to merge with the
residue of the Picts, so that even today one is conscious of the
'Kingdom's' special character, and this includes architecture.

A Fife laird, it is said, 'has a puckle o' land, a lump o' debt, a
doocot and a law plea'. This probably refers mainly to what have
been called 'blue-bonnet lairds', a term thought to have been
invented by Scott to describe a laird who was not actually a feudal
baron, as he wasn't, but in any case, there were and indeed still
are a number of modest properties in Fife and a number of
families who have been there for a very long time, especially in
the East Neuk, around Anstruther. It was here, in the eighteenth
century, that a ribald and obscene club known as 'the Beggar's
Benison' was formed, 'to which every laird from Cambo to Largo
belonged, without exception'.

Of the genuinely old and baronial Fife families one of the oldest
were the Duries, who were associated with Dunfermline Abbey

Rossend 'Castle', Burntisland, Fife

both in medieval times and at the dawn of the Reformation and had their country retreat in a manor house now called Rossend 'Castle', at Burntisland, along the coast.

Rossend 'Castle' was the subject of a protracted and bitter controversy a few years ago. It stood derelict and visibly collapsing, the prey of youthful and other vandals, and the local council wished to demolish it, to save the ratepayers' money, they said. Then in the course of a particular vandalistic visitation a ceiling fell down to reveal some superb painted beams which, protected under a century or two of plaster, had retained much of their pristine Jacobean colour and appearance. The fight to save the old house of the Duries took on a new complexion, and in the end a firm of architects bought Rossend and, with the aid of a grant from the Historic Buildings Council of Scotland, restored it as their offices. The ceiling was taken down before this and re-erected as part of an exhibition devoted to 'Painting in Scotland (1570–1650)' in the Scottish National Portrait Gallery in Edinburgh. It was set in its period and so has remained ever since, cleaned and cared for. What a pity this could not have been done in several other cases, and particularly with the two armorial ceilings at Collairnie, in North Fife, which show the arms of most of the Old Fife Families as they existed in the late sixteenth century, and notably those who were connected by marriage with the Barclays, whose baronial seat Collairnie was.

Collairnie Tower, North Fife

The Barclays were yet another Norman family on their way further north, and these ceilings at Collairnie are part of their story, told in heraldry. As yet neither the Historic Buildings people nor the National Trust for Scotland have been able to do much to rescue them from further deterioration. The trouble is that the tower house in which they are rises from the midst of cow byres; in fact, one has to go past the bull to get in at all! If they had been fifty yards to the north, east or west, the place would have been saved ages ago. Until now the farmer has not been the owner, while the latter has not been prepared to disturb him for the sake of these rare paintings, though one would have thought they could, as in the case of Rossend, be removed to a safer place, restored and put on show? The family of Barclay eventually established themselves in Aberdeenshire and at Towie Barclay built another tower house. One of them also made a name for himself as a general in the army of the Tsar, as the famous Barclay de Tolly who defeated Napoleon in 1812. A long way from Berkeley

Jacobean Gothic Hall at Towie Barclay, Aberdeenshire

Castle, in Gloucestershire, whence the first of the family emigrated north with Queen Margaret, and a long way too from Towie Barclay. The 'Tolly' perhaps derives from Towie or the other way round?

Towie Barclay has recently been restored, by the aid of a grant, by a former pop singer, and nicely too. It is unfortunate that in the course of time the two upper storeys have gone, and the rest of the building has been used as farm steadings. The remarkable thing about Towie Barclay, however, is its vaulted Jacobean version of a 'Gothycke' hall. R. W. Billings, in his splendid book from which we illustrate the hall in question, was taken in, as many others have been, by this fine place. The old timber floors were replaced by stone in Jacobean times, and in doing so the greater ease and comparative prosperity of the times permitted more elaboration, as here.

Slightly south of Towie Barclay, at Balbegno, on the border of Angus and Kincardineshire, there is another, contemporary vaulted hall, but this time the decoration is painted, on stone, not sculptured. Not a very satisfactory way of doing things, and the place is not so well preserved in consequence. Balbegno belongs to Sir William Gladstone, descendant of the great Prime Minister Gladstone, and is joined to, and in part used as, a farmhouse, though treated with respect.

The painted ceilings at Rossend were put in by the second Sir Robert Melville (there were two, father and son), reputedly for the return to Scotland of James VI and I in 1617. In fact, the King never came here, but their excellence and up-to-dateness, showing all the Jacobean fables and heroic legends, seem to suggest an importance the house and its owners did not them-selves quite possess. It is true, of course, that Mary, Queen of Scots, did visit Rossend on a progress to St Andrews, on which occasion the poet Châtelard for the second time secreted himself in her bedroom, so annoying the Queen that she ordered her step-brother, Lord James Stewart, Earl of Moray, to kill him on the spot. In fact, Châtelard was tried before a court in St Andrews and executed there, but not before he had recited appropriate poems about cruel and beautiful princesses. This was in 1563 before the Melvilles were granted the barony in 1588, the Duries having been displaced at the Reformation. They turned up again elsewhere, and at Durie House, near Leven, is the only sizeable

Earlshall, Fife

Georgian mansion in Fife, together with a very fine classical doocot. The Melvilles have also long since departed, at least from Rossend, but their splendid baronial pew in the kirk at Burntisland, richly carved and painted, has survived intact and has become what is called 'the magistrates' pew', though it is actually the pulpit of the church.

Before we leave painted ceilings in Fife, a word about the long gallery at Earlshall, north of St Andrews. This gallery, decorated in a mixture of heraldry, slogans and symbolic figures, but in *grisaille*, was rescued from dereliction towards the end of the nineteenth century, when it was painstakingly restored and partially repainted under the guidance of Sir Robert Lorimer. The building is a typical Z-plan with a round tower at one end and a square one at the other, joined to a further tower by a courtyard wall and enclosing a now famous topiary garden. This was the creation of the architect on what was at the time a ploughed field. Earlshall was Lorimer's first solo job and in many ways his best restoration, for, although his client more or less gave him *carte blanche* and supplied ample funds, and the architect was able to try out several of his own special ideas, he was less fanciful than on later commissions, and the work was more of a genuine restoration than a re-creation. At the end of the long gallery the owner's dog was depicted above the fireplace, and this was painted out by the next proprietor, only to be re-discovered by the latest, who, I'm told, thinks it original. He also calls the house Earlshall Castle. This is much more off the mark, since the local castle was Leuchars and built by the de Quincys in pre-Bannockburn days. It fell to the Carnegies, who disposed of it several centuries later, and it is now represented by a few lumps and bumps in a field to the north on the road to Dundee.

Earlshall, which dates in part from the sixteenth century and in part from the seventeenth, was the creation of the Bruce family, whose arms and monograms can be seen in the building. It was so named after the mythical thanes or earls of Fife of whom there had not been any since the Middle Ages but whose title was re-created in the eighteenth century for the Elgin banker, Mr Duff. He lent money to the government to fight Prince Charles Edward, became an earl and built Duff House, at Banff, replete with fake ancestral tombs nearby. One of his descendants married a daughter of Edward VII and became Duke of Fife, though strictly speaking this was not territorial. The traditional redoubt of the thanes of Fife was Macduff Castle, near Wemyss, on the shores of the Firth of Forth.

It is a moot point which is the oldest Old Fife Family. Some would say the Dishingtons, who, however, with the Duries, have disappeared from the scene. Many of the most ancient and interesting documents regarding the granting of lands and endowing of churches bear their signature and seal. They lived at Ardross between Elie and St Monans, where the beautiful pre-Reformation kirk was certainly closely associated with them, but nothing much more remains of their seat than of Leuchars Castle. Happily Ardross doocot has survived, has been restored and is preserved. It has its own protecting fence and wicket gate beside Ardross Farm and can be visited at any time.

These doocots were very important: they were not only status symbols, being permitted only to certain lairds by royal approval, but provided winter feeding, the birds being allowed to range over the land of lesser mortals, even lesser lairds. There were

Doocot at Ardross, East Neuk o'Fife

about three hundred in Fife at one time, now a few less than a third of that number, but the fact that they have survived at all shows how strong the old superstition is that one should not pull down a doocot. I have known two to be pulled down recently but one of these was certainly removed by a club, not a particular person. It was James VI, always superstitious about anything, who decreed it illegal to remove a doocot, and the link between royal command and wizardry probably accounts for so many still

standing, damaged but there, in the fields and occasionally near the house for whose benefit they were first erected.

The Dishingtons have gone, but within sight of Ardross is Balcaskie, and on either side of it are Elie and Anstruther, all connected with the Italian–Norman family of de Candela, which

Bruce's doocot, Kinross House

came to Fife in the eleventh century and is still there. The Candelas settled first in Anstruther, where they had three different houses at different times. The first may have been where Dreel 'Castle' now is, on the banks of the Dreel Burn as it enters the sea, and it was probably there that Charles II had his good dinner in a 'crow's nest'. They also had a house further up the burn and in the seventeenth century acquired the building known as 'the Watchtower', which was built at the end of the

Georgian doocot at Durie House, Fife

sixteenth century by the minister, James Melville, and left by him to his son, who sold it to the Anstruthers. It became for a while a dower house, but there were others, notably a tall town house at Pittenweem harbour with the laird's kennels for foxhounds behind, and two grander seats, at Balcaskie and Elie.

North front, Balcaskie, Fife

Balcaskie is sometimes described as the first mansion house built in Scotland—that is, presumably, a building of regular architecture and not either a tall tower house or a long 'palas'. It was the home of Sir William Bruce, Architect Royal to Charles II and one of those on the secret council which visited that monarch in Holland during the Commonwealth and helped his return. Balcaskie was then in the possession of another member of the same secret council, Sir Thomas Moncreiffe of that Ilk, who sold it to Bruce. It was through this connection that the King's Architect got the commission to design Moncreiffe House, near Perth, which was, really, the first mansion house in Scotland. It was purely Palladian and served as the model for Bruce's own larger mansion, at Kinross, in the same style.

Balcaskie already existed when William Bruce came to it, and it was here that he tried out a scheme which he was to employ on several existing buildings which had to be enlarged, notably Holyrood, where he copied the existing old bit, a slight distance away, then joined them with a regular frontispiece. Bruce bought Kinross twenty years before he left Balcaskie and the Anstruthers came to live there. He and his son planted the Kinross estate and completed the stable wing before the house had reached its ground floor. He was a great believer in tradition, so unusual for a Palladian architect, most of whom had no respect for the past unless it was Greek or Roman. Thus, since Kinross was in the barony of Loch Leven, in whose castle Mary, Queen of

'Italian' terrace at Balcaskie

Scots, had been imprisoned a century earlier, he had an armorial stone from the castle inserted as a keystone in one of his new garden gazebos, so as to express architecturally the sense of continuity. Whilst still at Balcaskie he put in some splendid fretwork ceilings, bringing the royal gentlemen plasterers over from Holyrood to make them. These ceilings, or rather the taste for them, spread north as far as the Moray Firth, as we shall see, though few were by the same experts whom Bruce employed and who had been sent north specially by the King after decorating the State Apartments at Windsor.

Bruce also laid out the 'Italian' terrace at Balcaskie and imported the busts of Roman emperors into the Fife landscape, planting trees in avenues and creating vistas in the grand manner. One of these opens directly from the main windows of his house right across the Firth of Forth to the Bass Rock. It is likely there were once three such vistas, the other two going to the May Isle and Berwick Law respectively.

Balcaskie has only just become the principal seat of the

Anstruthers; formerly it was Elie House, which has not so happy an architectural history or position. There was probably an L-shaped tower there once, but apart from an amusing bit of Baroque swagger around one window on the south side, possibly the work of William Adam, the main façade is dull and unin-

Stable entrance and datestone,
Donibristle, Fife

spiring. It was almost certainly the work of Alexander MacGill, architect to the city of Edinburgh and a follower of Bruce, though lacking the master's imagination or skill. William Adam shows a more grandiose design of his own in *Vitruvius Scoticus*, and Sir James Clerk of Penicuik also made a sketch for a proposed main façade, but neither of these was carried out.

The Anstruthers left Elie more than a century ago, but not before they also left the delightful story of Lady Janet, whose Folly, the so-called 'Lady's Tower', can be seen on the edge of the sea just beyond the town. The story is that when Janet (who was a 'lady' only by marriage) went bathing, a man rang a little bell to warn onlookers off, and she had the tower arranged with steps down so she could go into the water at high or low tide.

Alexander MacGill was much more successful at Donibristle,

Wrought ironwork, Donibristle House

further along the coast towards Queensferry. The site there was very much finer, facing right onto the Firth of Forth with a splendid panorama towards Edinburgh, Arthur's Seat and the Lothian Hills. There had been a castle in much the same position before, which was burnt down, and this had been the scene of the murder of the second Earl of Moray, son-in-law of the Regent Moray, assassinated in the streets of Linlithgow in 1591. This latter was the 'Bonnie Earl o' Moray' of the somewhat lengthy ballad, whose lustiness and handsome looks had attracted the attention of Queen Anne of Denmark, so that when he was murdered, her husband, James VI, told the family not to try to pursue his murderers. He was, in any case, suspected of being privy to one of the numerous plots, real and unreal, by which the jittery King felt himself threatened.

MacGill's house was very Bruce-like, with central building flanked on either side by pavilions linked to the centre, while down to the sea steps and terraces led, lined with the most superb wrought ironwork in Scotland. Of all this only one pavilion and the ironwork survives. There was another fire in the nineteenth century, and although the present Earl of Moray tells me they spent short spells there off and on until the 1950s, none of them has been back since. The property was leased to the Royal Navy, who painted the wrought iron white, which, one supposes, was only to be expected in the light of the 'If it moves, salute it; if it doesn't, paint it' dictum; but even they have now gone, and the whole place is a mess. A commuters housing estate encroaches almost daily, but because the buildings are protected they are not demolished, only allowed to fall down. The stables were actually designed by Bruce, and there is also a decrepid, almost unrecognizable chapel. What is still there is that marvellous ironwork. It was almost certainly done by foreigners, but whether in Holland, as is sometimes said, and brought over whole and ready to be fixed, or by craftsmen working in the south is not certain.

When Louis XIV revoked the Edict of Nantes, which gave freedom of worship to French Protestants, many Huguenot craftsmen went to live in Holland, and these included not just jewellers, furniture-makers and sculptors but ironworkers. Amongst them was Jean Tijou, who subsequently came with others to England in the train of William of Orange, and Tijou did the grilles in the choir of St Paul's Cathedral and the grilles and gates to the park at Hampton Court. The ironwork at Donibristle is quite the equal of any of this, and it is hoped it will be either properly looked after soon or else removed before it gets too damaged.

The earls of Moray rejoice under a secondary title of lords of St Colme. This is the St Colme's Isle of Shakespeare's *Macbeth*, and the Inchcolm of Fife, since St Columba had a monastery on the island. At the Reformation its monastic buildings were preserved, but not the church, which was pulled down for its stone; they became the baronial seat of the Douglas earls of Morton. They subsequently moved to the mainland at Aberdour and enlarged and improved the castle there. This is now a ruin in the care of the Department of the Environment, though a later addition, completely domestic and indistinguishable from a decent house in the street, is the caretaker's lodge. The grounds have been tidied up as a public park with walled garden and an old bowling green; there is a fine 'beehive' doocot, and the chapel has been restored as a place of public worship.

The Mortons, like the earls of Moray, had royal connections of a sort, and the first Earl, Regent of the kingdom and a somewhat shifty individual, was eventually tried and executed for High Treason. He was one of those implicated in one of the two, or possible three, concurrent plots to murder Lord Darnley. His reason was that the Queen's husband was suspected of planning the re-introduction of Roman Catholicism into Scotland; Bothwell simply wanted to get rid of his rival, while the Queen's reason, if she had one, was that she wanted to marry Bothwell! In any event, Darnley went up in smoke at Kirk o' Fields, but only after he had already been stabbed to death on behalf of someone else. Morton produced the so-called 'Casket Letters' that appeared to blame the Queen, but it does not seem likely she would want her husband out of the way while she was pregnant, even if the child wasn't his. The whole thing was most unsavoury, and Mary, Queen of Scots part, whatever it was, gave Elizabeth Tudor an excuse for receiving her badly in England and locking her up; or was it jealousy?

Morton's nephew who succeeded him was the unfortunate Queen's gaoler in Loch Leven Castle, but his son was the brave lad who got hold of the keys and rowed her to safety. After that the family showed an ever-increasing attachment to the Stuarts and during the Civil War the then Earl lent Charles I £100,000, which even in Scots money was a lot at the time. Subsequent earls married into English families, including that of the Duke of Buckingham, and one was a prime mover in getting the Act of Union through the Scottish Parliament in 1707. Thus, when Aberdour Castle, even with additions, became insufficiently comfortable and up-to-date, they abandoned it for a pleasant new manor house nearby, the Place of Aberdour, orange washed and roofed in lovely old sepia tiles, plain but nicely proportioned. On the lawn in front is a beautiful Baroque sundial showing on one side the Douglas Heart and on another the insignia of the Order of the Garter, which, almost uniquely for a Scotsman, the Earl held.

Neither the Douglases nor the Stewarts could be called Fifers; both came from the west, the former not even part of the Norman ascendancy in origin, while the Stewarts, who had been High Stewards to the kings of Scots for two centuries, did arrive in the north as attendants of David I, but via Wales and Brittany. The Lindsays, on the other hand, are very much an OFF: their head, the Earl of Crawford and Balcarres, is the premier earl of

Sundial, Place of Aberdour, Fife

Scotland. The Fife branch hailed from Balcarres, which estate almost marches with that of Balcaskie, and they have given Scotland some of its most romantic and attractive history.

It is a pity Balcarres House has been so altered and spoilt down the ages. Surrounded by and encased within two nasty additions, one in the Gothic revival of the beginning of last century and a larger baronial one by Bryce made later in the same era, is a tiny corner of the old tower house of the Lindsays, their baronial seat. It is all there, actually, but inside out, so to speak. It was the home of Colin Lindsay, third Earl of Balcarres, who, a courtier to Charles II, ended his life in genial but definitive custody on his own estate here. He had 'been out' for King James at the end of the seventeenth century and again for his son, the 'King over the Water' in the early eighteenth, and would have been imprisoned with other 'rebels' but for the intervention of the Duke of Marlborough, who was a friend of his; so he spent his old age in the company of an English dragoon, who accompanied him everywhere he went. He founded the village of Colinsburgh, in the reign of Queen Anne, so he is not forgotten; if he should be, there is always that fake tower on Balcarres Craig, not built by him but

North façade at Innergellie House, East Neuk o'Fife

which might very well have been; it combines the ivy-clad shivers of the Gothic revival with a feel for old Caledonia.

Balcarres was very Jacobite; one of the older rooms is that called after Bishop David Low, who, in the days of the penal laws, when non-jurors were not allowed to preach to more than five persons at a time, held services there. There is also a burial chapel in the grounds which dates from this period and which was copied in part when the penal laws were withdrawn and Bishop Low founded the little church of St John in Pittenweem. It was the same bishop who lived in the priory there and in 1822, having become a latter-day establishmentarian, read the address of welcome to George IV at Holyroodhouse.

The Lumsdaines, or Lumsdens, cannot be left out of this narrative either. Unlike the Lindsays and Anstruthers, who are still very much *in situ* in Fife, they departed some years ago, but in this century. Their manor, on the other hand, is very hale and much appreciated by its present occupant, a lady whose husband headed the firm that built the 'Queens' on Clydebank. Innergellie House is L-shaped but was improved in the late seventeenth and early eighteenth centuries and possesses a perfectly magnificent, if slightly gauche, northern façade. This is all pediments and pilasters and obviously the work of a genuine amateur—I use the word in its dictionary meaning, a 'lover' but not necessarily an expert.

One used to think, incorrectly, that this extraordinary front,

Renaissance tombs of the Lumsdaines
in Crail kirkyard

which reminded one of the Renaissance part of the Schloss at Heidelberg, was the inspiration of old General Lumsdaine, who with others from Scotland went to the wars on the continent of Europe in the service of Gustavus Adolphus and after Lutzen came back and fought for the highest bidders here, King or Covenanters. Lumsdaine will be remembered by Civil War writers as the man who drew the map of the battle scene at Marston Moor, and this has survived for their delectation—indeed, it is reproduced in Brigadier Peter Young's definitive record of that fateful fight in which the Scots played such a decisive part in the defeat of Prince Rupert. There is a fine double doocot in the grounds at Innergellie, and Lumsden tombs in the kirkyard. There are more and finer ones, in that exuberant Renaissance style that was certainly brought here from either Germany or Sweden in the seventeenth century, in the kirkyard at Crail, to the east.

The Hopes are an Old Fife Family only by adoption. There is a monument in 'the Kingdom' to one of them dating from the time of the Peninsular War in which the then Earl of Hopetoun played a prominent part, and there used to be an older memorial to their sojourn in 'the Kingdom' at Craighall, which was their baronial seat when they settled in Scotland after a century in Holland. Craighall, which stood on the outskirts of Fife's reputedly bonniest village, Ceres, was dynamited in the 1950s as unsafe, having been given up by the Hopes and left to decay and crumble.

This question of demolition and when it is legitimate is a vexed one. The regulations say one must not take chimneypieces, panelling and other objects out of an existing ancient building except in special circumstances, and recently the Earl of Seafield was prevented from selling even some Victorian ones from Cullen House, though it was empty and he no longer lived there. Nor is it allowable to make additions to protected buildings; nor, apparently, though again there seem to be exceptions, can one remove a wing, a tower, a lean-to of any antiquity. What of total demolition? A fairly large number of historic buildings have been demolished in recent years, and on enquiry one is told that, provided the demolishers advertise in the Press, the fact they intend to demolish and provided no one objects within three weeks, they can do it. I don't think even that stipulation held when Craighall was blown up, and all that now remains of the *caput* of this barony is a stone eagle, which Lord Linlithgow rescued and has put up on a gatepost at Hopetoun House, in West Lothian.

The original Craighall was a Fife laird's tower, but the Hopes rose quickly in the world. James, younger son of Sir Thomas Hope of Craighall, became Governor of the Mint and a Lord of Session under Charles I, and it was his son who began the building of Hopetoun House, the so-called 'Versailles of Scotland'. Sir Thomas's heir married Anne Bruce, daughter of William Bruce the architect, and it was through this connection that Craighall was enlarged by the King's Architect. The latter later designed the original Hopetoun House, subsequently enlarged and altered by the Adam family, *pere et fils*, and only finally completed in time for a state visit by 'Prinney' a century later. At Craighall Bruce joined two separate towers, as he loved doing, with a superb arched feature with semi-circular pediment, possibly the first pedimented centrepiece seen in Scotland, though not far off he made a small triangular one at Wemysshall, which, like this one, is no more.

If we follow the Hopes to West Lothian, we also follow their associates, of course: Bruce at work at Holyrood for the Duke of

Staneyhill Tower, West Lothian

Lauderdale and the King, for instance. We find on the Hopetoun estate Staneyhill Tower, seat of Sir William Sharpe, the Royal Cashkeeper and the man who paid Bruce and the craftsmen employed at the palace. The tower was L-shaped but unusual in having strap-work quoins which were almost certainly taken from the ornamental cornerstones at Heriot's Hospital, in Edinburgh, the finest Renaissance building in the capital. The tower has long since become a folly and is ruined, but the Sharpes, or Shairps, have links in the district and also, curiously enough, with Fife. Archbishop Sharpe of St Andrews was murdered in the presence of his pleading daughter on Magus Muir by a group of Covenanters armed with both pistols and swords, which they used continuously to display their venom and hatred for the man who, formerly a Presbyterian, had allowed himself to be consecrated a bishop and become Primate of Scotland.

The principal seat of the Sharpes was Houstoun, some miles to the west of Staneyhill. This a tall, five-storeyed house, each floor showing diminishing window sizes, and the rooms reached via a

Houston House, West Lothian: note doocot

comfortable eighteenth-century stair. There used to be only a spiral but it was replaced when the decoration of the interior was modernized according to contemporary standards—with nice French-grey painted panelling, for instance, now camouflaged. The lower floors are vaulted and to the north is a small back courtyard where once were the bakehouse, brewhouse and servants' quarters, the latter reached via an outside stair. Houstoun was acquired by Ian Lindsay, the architect, from the Sharpes complete with ancestral portraits and some of the furniture. He lived there and also used part as his office. It was there that he initiated the listing and categorizing of Scotland's ancient buildings, using as a basis his own remarkable card index collection of postcards and photos which he left to the Scottish National Monuments Records Office when he died.

There are no signs of any kind of defence at Houstoun, not even a shut-hole; it was purely domestic from its first erection in the seventeenth century. It is obvious from this that in that comparatively progressive era life was much more secure in the Lothians than beyond, especially in the north, where they were

Philpstoun House, West Lothian, *c.*1680

still erecting towers of defence with gunloops and look-outs, some decorative, it is true, but not all, the enemy in these regions being one's own neighbours. Nowadays things are getting back to this in some quarters, so one shouldn't laugh too loudly at the tricks our Jacobean ancestors got up to to defend themselves from vandals and thieves, when there was no police force and the royal writ, as interpreted by a combination of the remaining feudal barons and the sheriff courts, did not always carry much weight.

Philpstoun is another totally domestic manor house in the vicinity but, instead of being tall and narrow like Houstoun, is a handsome two-bayed edifice of almost Home Counties charm and refinement. It was built some fifty years later, but its crow-steps give it away as Scottish, and it is harled. Otherwise it sits down so calmly one would never know it was the seat of a Dundas of Dundas whose martial tower is not far away. John Dundas of Philpstoun was the builder; his initials and those of his wife, plus the date 1676, appear in the midst of some strapwork decoration over the central window on the ground floor. The house's main attractions, apart from its site, in green pastures and woods, with double doocot in attendance, are six sundials, one on each corner of the building between the levels of the lower and upper windows. The stairs are also typical of their date, no longer spiral or hidden in the thickness of the walls but scale-and-platt—that is, up with landing, and round again and up again, and set in their own projecting bay at the back.

The Dundases brought Carmelite friars to Scotland and settled them at Queensferry, nearby, where they built the little fortified kirk which today is the only former Carmelite foundation in Britain still used as a church. At the Reformation it was spared on account of its being a private establishment, and the friars were allowed to die out in peace. After a period it fell into disuse, and it was rescued only towards the end of last century, through the initiative of the Dundases and Bishop Dowden of Edinburgh, when John Kinross was called in to restore it. Kinross was not an architect *per se* but an artist; he was Secretary of the Royal Scottish Academy but noted for his scholarly restorations of Greyfriars, in Elgin, and Falkland Palace, in Fife.

Almost within sight, actually within sight in winter, of Philpstoun, is Midhope, called a castle and possibly containing the nucleus of one at its westernmost end. It lies on the Hopetoun estate, and the late Marquis of Linlithgow, Viceroy of India, had plans for its restitution. Alas, during the war it was handed over to the tender mercies of the Fire Service, and when they had finished with their axes, ladders and hoses, the place was not much use to anyone. The weather quickly got in and the fine late-Stuart panelling, and staircase with barley-sugar balusters, had to be removed and burnt on account of woodworm. Then the roof began to fall in, and finally the farmer, unable to get his machinery through the classical gateway to Midhope's court-yard, bashed down the wall on one side. There is a maximum fine of £200 for the wanton demolishing of protected buildings but even if it was imposed, as it surely should have been here, it could scarcely be considered a proper deterrent for this sort of vandalism. Midhope belonged to the Livingstones, who were Hereditary Keepers of the Key at Linlithgow Palace and earls of that name. They died out at the beginning of the eighteenth century, and the present Marquis of Linlithgow, who is a Hope, rejoices in a re-created title.

Midhope consists of the remnants of an older tower to which is

Callendar House, Falkirk

joined a house. It possesses a fine classical doorway with the insignia of the third Livingstone Earl of Linlithgow over it, plus over-sailed turrets at the 'castle' end. This means the conical caps that once roofed the turrets have been sliced off and the slates brought down over. It was a common practice when towers and castles were enlarged, though something a great deal more drastic was done in the case of Callendar House, the Livingstone seat near Falkirk. Mary Livingstone was one of the 'Four Maries', the others being Mary Seton, Mary Beaton and Mary Fleming, who as little girls accompanied the four-year-old Mary, Queen of Scots, to France and stayed with her into adult life. In the old Callendar House, entirely enveloped in the new, the marriage agreement between Mary Stuart and the Dauphin François was signed.

Early in the eighteenth century came the first enlargement, when the Livingstones married into the Callendars, but this was nothing to what happened between 1869 and 1877, when the architects Wardrop and Reid were employed to create what was then said to be the largest mansion of its kind in Britain, and

Kinneil House, Bo'ness, a Hamilton seat

which, although ostensibly in the style of Francis I of France, is more on the scale of something suitable for, say, the Empress Eugenie to have retired to on the fall of the Second Empire. Its future, though still in doubt, is more assured than it was a few years ago, when the Provost of Falkirk declared it reminded him of the days of slavery and should be pulled down. One would have thought it could have made an excellent Civic or Cultural Centre.

In order to gain the approval of the Regent of Scotland, the Earl of Arran (himself related to the royal house and ambitious for his own son to marry the Queen), to the union between the Dauphin and the infant Mary Stuart, the title of Duc de Châtelhérault was bestowed on him. He then proceeded to erect a mansion for himself at Kinneil, on a spur above the Firth of Forth between Queensferry and Falkirk. Becoming afterwards a supporter of the Queen, he subsequently found himself out of favour, and in due course the Earl of Morton destroyed his house at Kinneil.

That might have been the end of the story altogether, but in the next century, in the days of Anne, Duchess of Hamilton in her

The House of the Binns, West Lothian, baronialized in 1825

own right, a new Kinneil was built out of the remnants of the Earl of Arran's mansion. It was added to on the south by a large five-storeyed Restoration centrepiece, complete with galleried balustrading and square-capped side pavilions, in imitation of Bruce's at Balcaskie, and approached via a long and wide avenue. Fate has not dealt kindly with this addition any more than it did with the first. It is set in a rather dreary public park, its avenue gone and where vandalism is almost uncontrollable, though happily the Renaissance wall decorations which have been found in the Earl of Arran's wing are well protected by the Ancient Monuments people. They are amongst the best preserved in Scotland and of a very high standard, as perhaps befits their origin.

The Earl's French properties were near Poitiers, and in the nineteenth century his descendant the then Duke of Abercorn tested his title in the French courts, it being upheld. Oddly enough, not long afterwards, Napoleon III, whose former flame and cousin, Princess Marie of Baden, married another branch of the Hamilton family, created a new dukedom of Châtelhérault for his cousin's husband, and this is still held by the present Duke of Hamilton, so that there are two Ducs de Châtelhérault in Scotland, one royal, the other imperial.

Almost as much camouflaged by later additions as Callendar House, only in a mock Tudor style, is The Binns, back on the border of the Hopetoun estate. Inside the considerable external castellations of the first half of the nineteenth century a suite of Carolean rooms survives on the upper floors of the U-shaped structure. It was never a tall tower house, but the seat of General Tam Dalyell, who was the son of a rich merchant who wished to display his newly acquired feudal status architecturally. This he did in at least three rooms which the first Scottish 'Pevsner', dealing with *The Lothians*, says 'embody the theory, if not the actual functions, of feudal loyalty'.

The rooms in question are the High Hall, the so-called King's Room and the Vaulted Chamber, and presumably they represent in symbolic form the manorial hall, the lord's solar and his bed-chamber? In any event, they are elaborately and interestingly plastered in the style of the period, *circa* 1630, the High Hall with central pendant, flowery frieze and appropriate heraldry, the latter honouring both the King and the Dalyells. The King's Room may refer either to the Biblical monarch whose head is represented, one of a series of heroes, Classical, Jewish and Christian, that adorned ceilings throughout Scotland in the early seventeenth century, or to the hope that the King himself, perhaps Charles I, who was crowned at Holyrood in 1633, might come and sleep there. The Vaulted Chamber is different, on account not only of its low vault but of its strapwork, which is not dissimilar from that in a room in Moray House, in Edinburgh, which itself was probably inspired by work done for King James VI and I's homecoming in 1617, when Edinburgh Castle was 'modernized'.

The General who commissioned the decoration of The Binns was so devoted to the Stuarts that on the beheading of Charles I he swore he would grow a beard and not cut it until Charles II was restored. This he did, till it came below his waist and he tucked it under his belt. During the Commonwealth he went to Russia and fought for the Tsar, and it was whilst there that he got the idea, from the Russian winter uniform, for the Scots Greys, which he founded on his return. His boots can be seen in The Binns. He was much feared and hated by the Covenanters, whom he routed at Rullion Green; because they thought they had God on their side, and yet lost, they attributed Tam's victory to an alliance with the Devil.

Hopetoun aisle, Abercorn kirk, West Lothian

There are at least two amusing stories on this subject: the first that the numerous turrets at The Binns were put there to make it more difficult for the Devil, with whom the General quarrelled, to pull it down; the second says that Tam defeated the Devil at cards, whereupon the latter threw a white marble table-top at him in a fury. Certainly The Binns is well turreted and battlemented, but not in a style General Dalyell would have recognized; while there is a white marble table-top lying in the park where one is told it landed some time in the second half of the seventeenth century.

The Binns was the first historic house of its kind presented to the National Trust of Scotland, by Mrs Eleanor Dalyell, who continued to live there until her recent death. Her son, a twentieth-century 'Tam', is Member of Parliament for West Lothian and has a flat in the house. He may be a bit sceptical about some of the legends surrounding his famous forebear, but it remains true that at Abercorn kirk, on the Hopetoun estate, where the Dalyells have their family aisle (combined burial place and baronial pew), they may not enter the body of the kirk but face across it, away from the Hopes, whose 'box' faces the congregation from behind the Communion Table, thus ensuring they are seen, if not worshipped! I restored the Hopes aisle and 'Box' some years ago. It consists of a classical addition at one side of the church, with tombs below and upstairs a series of retiring rooms so that the family could have a cold lunch between sermons and then return to their high-level pew at the east end for a second dose in the afternoon. It represents the acme of feudal superiority in Scotland and, dating from the beginning of the eighteenth century (it was actually the last design of an aged Sir William Bruce), shows how long and how lasting is the lairdly tradition. On the coved ceiling behind the Hopes is their armorial achievement painted by Richard Waitt, the principal artist for such in the reign of Queen Anne.

4.   From Baronial to Renaissance

At the very time when lairds in the south were getting rid of their turrets and shot-holes, coming down from their tower houses and building more comfortable, less aggressive-looking homes for themselves, the north saw the apogee of the native adaptation of the Norman keep in a series of superb castles in the valleys of the Don and the Dee, particularly the latter. This part of the country is half Highland and half Lowland, perhaps two-thirds the latter, and includes, besides a slice of Kincardineshire which is wholly Lowland, the district known as Mar.

The so-called 'Castles of Mar' are, of course, famous and have been written up and photographed a good deal already, but since most of them are also the seats of feudal barons and are, in any case, integral to an understanding of the development of the Scottish Baronial style, one must say something more here. The oldest is Drum, its early fourteenth-century, possibly late thirteenth-century, tower almost certainly the oldest one of its kind in Scotland—in use, that is, for the erstwhile Lord's Hall has been adapted as a library, and the only noticeable alteration outside has been the enlargement of a window and the permanent placing of steps up to the first floor. These would have been movable in times past. The tower was built at royal instigation to guard the Caledonian Forest, part of which still survives, for hunting and the preservation of game were most important to Scotland's rulers and their baronial servants; and not only game, for the wilder animals had also to be kept down and prevented from terrorizing the neighbourhood. My records tell me, for instance, that in 1564, when the Earl of Atholl entertained Mary, Queen of Scots, to a hunt, the bag consisted not only of over three hundred red deer but of five wolves.

Drum Castle, Aberdeenshire: the manor house with a corner of the old
tower

People in the south tend to look askance at hunting, and I noticed in the book *English Manor Houses* that the word sport in this context was put in inverted commas. I suppose this is all right in a highly urbanized setting, where there are too many people, too many houses and very little real country, but not so obvious up here. At any rate, Mar is still a great hunting ground, of royalty as well as others, and the Castle at Midmar, as we have seen, was probably given to a friend of Sir William Wallace as a hunting lodge. The kings of Scots were great lovers of the chase and had hunting properties in a number of areas. Boar Hills, in Fife, is well known, and the name tells its own story, while not far away, at Falkland, both Mary, Queen of Scots, and her son, James VI and I, hunted whenever they could get away from the cares of state. Traquair too began life as a royal hunting lodge, and the northernmost corner of the manor house may very well represent one of the earliest such erections, vying with Drum, in Aberdeenshire, as to date.

Drum, unlike almost all the other 'Castles of Mar', did not become turreted and almost top heavy with ornament and false defensive features. The Irvines, who were guardians, with the Burnetts at Crathes, of the Royal Forest, built a brand new annexe in the form of a late Jacobean mansion house, and that is where they lived until a few years ago, when the last laird in the main line presented the property to the National Trust for Scotland. There was some comment about this at the time because, apparently, there were quite a few Irvine descendants only too anxious and willing to take over, and in such a case the family is probably as important as the building, let alone the contents, which have usually been accumulated by a number of people and not just by the existing owner. Elsewhere properties have gone to the Trust when the laird has had no descendant, or none willing to take over, and that is understandable, especially where the baronial seat has belonged to the same family since the beginning and the contents are integral to it.

Recently it seemed that a solution to the first dilemma had been found in the creation of the National Heritage Memorial Fund, a Government body that so far had not been put to the test, or was not until the proprietor of Thirlestane Castle, in the Borders, approached them for help. This nearly hundred-roomed pile, formerly the seat of the Duke of Lauderdale, had already been restored with the aid of a grant of some £400,000, when Captain Maitland-Carew realized he simply could not maintain the place any longer. He could not go to the National Trust, as they require an endowment. Accordingly he tried the new National Heritage Memorial Fund, with the result that, in exchange for the gift of

Crathes Castle, Kincardineshire, from the garden

most of the property, worth more than £1 million, Thirlestane now has an endowment in excess of £600,000 and the family remain in one wing, with a garden, thus preserving building, contents and historic associations.

Crathes went to the National Trust some years ago, and the Burnetts continued to live in one wing, the garden being, at that time, almost as celebrated and worth visiting as the castle.

Although on the north bank of the River Dee, we are here firmly in Kincardineshire, and in Lowland country, with the dower house of the family 'over the hill' by the sea, at Muchalls. This latter is still private property and little known, though it is open to the public on occasion and boasts some of the finest plaster ceilings hereabouts. The plasterers whom we met at The Binns, and whose first efforts were in Jacobean Edinburgh, came up north by stages, with their apprentices, stopping at Glamis *en route*. There the moulds seem to have been used as intended, and the caryatides on either side of the chimneypiece are well formed while the combined heraldry and foliage above show no deterioration. Slightly more amusing interpretations appear at Muchalls, and the moulds have been used with more abandon, but this little seaside manor house does retain the original colours

Muchalls, Kincardineshire: note barmkin wall

that must have adorned other plaster ceilings which are now all pristine white. Obviously the heraldry must be properly tinctured to have any meaning, as here, and as these ceilings originate in Italian Renaissance models the foliage and other features must also have been intended to be painted. Muchalls also boasts a miniature but complete barmkin wall enclosing the two open sides of its L-shape, making an attractive courtyard.

Now we come· to Midmar, whose baronal name was—and surely still is—Ballogie. Its builder was George Bell, whose tombstone survives in the kirkyard at Midmar and says he was the mason at 'Ballogy'. Until it was bought and 'done-up' by an 'Oily', Midmar, or Ballogie, had an enchantment all its own, an unreal feeling reminiscent of the dormant setting of *The Sleeping Princess*, waiting for the kiss that would bring the whole thing back to life, but not our life, another life, from the past. The last occupants before its recent sale were the Misses Gordon, in the nineteenth century, and inside the old house there still were a

Midmar, or Ballogie, Aberdeenshire

number of amusing souvenirs in the form of early water-closets, iron stoves and little seats by the windows so that pet dogs could see out. Ancient Monuments mention a 'medieval privy' in the grounds, and I well remember standing with Mrs Cleison Gordon, the key to Midmar in her hand, pointing out what was

Abergeldie, a Gordon barony on Deeside

obviously not a privy but a fountain. As she said, if one could get in, one certainly could not get out. Nearby was an old shed with an asbestos roof used for farm machinery, which she said was scheduled for preservation!

On the face of it Midmar has no great antiquity, dating as it stands almost entirely from the end of the sixteenth century, with a charming walled garden and a few later additions to the east, but some authorities speak of Ballogie having been given to a knightly companion of Sir William Wallace, rather like Drum and Crathes to the Irvines and Burnetts by Bruce, as a hunting lodge to guard the Caledonian Forest. If so, there is nothing to show for it. The Queen Mother visited the place shortly before she went to the Castle of Mey and was very tempted to come here. It would have been nearer Balmoral without being in sight of it, for this haven of peace, this manor house without apparent history and entirely unspoilt, faces away from the Dee, towards the Don. Her Majesty could have gone to Abergeldie, of course, which the royal family leased from the Gordons and which at one time was

Craigievar Castle, Aberdeenshire, Jacobean apotheosis of Scots Baronial

the Highland home of the Prince and Princess of Wales, afterwards Edward VII and Queen Alexandra, but she seems to have already half arranged to go to Caithness, miles away from everyone and everything.

Abergeldie is still virtually Lowland, although on the edge of the Balmoral estate, and was not bought by Prince Albert in 1848 with the rest of the property. It has recently been unleased and gone back to John Gordon of Abergeldie, who has restituted it with the help of an Historic Buildings grant and matriculated his baronial arms at the Lyon Court. It is not a large building, rectangualr in its main part with turret at one corner and stair tower at another, perhaps remarkable more for where it is than for anything else, a late sixteenth-century manor house in the

Great hall at Craigievar

upper Dee valley.

As a matter of fact, several Aberdeenshire castles and mansions are within sight of the Grampians, including Craigievar, which Douglas Simpson called a 'mountain *château*', and the Lowland barons had a constant fight with marauding Highlanders come in search of booty in the rich plain of Garioch, even after their bloody defeat at the Battle of Harlaw, in 1411, when Sir Alexander de Irwyne fought under the banner of St Columba against the Lord of the Isles and the Macleans of Duart.

If the castles of Mar as a group mark the apogee of the Scottish National style as a whole, surely Craigievar is their apotheosis? It was built all of a piece by an Aberdeen timber merchant as a status symbol, not a tower of defence, and this perhaps explains its near perfection. It is wholly of native inspiration and workmanship,

Bedchamber at Craigievar

134

DOE NOT WAKEN SLEIPING DOGS
D · F
16 68
Sheild on ye Staircase

except, possibly, for the plasterwork in the hall which was, in part at least, done by itinerant English plasterers with native apprentices, following earlier commissions in Edinburgh, Glamis and Muchalls. It has no garden or outbuildings of note to reduce the first dramatic impression as one approaches from the drive; indeed, it seems to rise directly from the ground, 'like a rocket', as one commentator has suggested, its conical turrets and ogee cupolas, crude balustrading and crow-steps, indented corbelling and decorative defences all at the top.

In Lord Sempill's day drive, harling and stonework were all the same colour, the pink of an old-fashioned tennis court, and few things had altered inside. There was no electricity or gas, oil lamps and candles sufficed, while not much more than a century ago rushes from the burn were still used to cover the floors and to provide wicks for the crusie lamps. It is not true, however, that nothing has changed since Willie the Merchant's time, for the downstairs windows have clearly been enlarged and all of them had sashes inserted, presumably in the eighteenth century, when the Baltic timber linings to some of the rooms were also put in. Originally the windows would have been either shutterboard, with fixed leaded lights above and opening wooden shutters below, or, as at Glamis still, fixed leaded lights above and opening lights below. Glamis is the only large Scottish mansion to retain these, which makes it all the more of a pity the frames have recently been painted white and not kept their old dark sepia appearance. This white business is a Victorian invention, part of the tidying up of old things to make them look new and tasteful. Woodwork should not be painted, if hardwood, and was usually stained to simulate hardwood if not. Inside too, this rule applied, though in the case of softwoods these were normally painted grey or blue-green, as at Holyrood and elsewhere where the colours have survived or been replaced.

When Craigievar was purchased by William Forbes in late Jacobean times, the property was described as the 'lands and baronies of Craigyvar with maynes-manor place . . . yeards, orchyeards, with corn and waulk milns, multures, sequels and knaveships yr of'. The latter were the homes of tenants who paid multures for the hire of the waulk milns, which they had literally to walk round to turn in those days but which later became horsegangs, where an animal performed this drudgery.

Castle Fraser, the first large Scottish *château*

The 'var' in Craigievar was corrupted from Mar, which was the name of the whole district. Thus, Castle Fraser, Craigievar's nearest rival for fame, is called after its owner, who was laird of Muchall-in-Mar. The Frasers came from Stirling and began to build with the rest at the end of the sixteenth century, but here the Bell family, who had already created Ballogie, or Midmar, were employed again, for 'I. Bell' is carved in the stonework of the Z-shaped castle which on plan closely resembles Midmar, Andrew Fraser, whom Charles I subsequently raised to the peerage and who repaid his sovereign by joining the Covenanters, was only a minor when he inherited the partially completed building, but it was he who made what we see today, the first real Scottish *château* in the French manner, a country house in all but detail.

In France there are few classical country houses, unlike England, which is the home *par excellence* of such things, and probably there would have been hardly any here in Scotland had the example of Fraser been followed and had Sir William Bruce not introduced the fully developed Palladian mode thirty years later. When the Earl of Strathmore and Kinghorne returned to his domains at the Restoration, he declared that the days of towers and battlements were quite over, and no one built in the old way any more. He was not absolutely correct, but more or less so, though curiously enough when he came to restore Glamis it was not on the Palladian model of Bruce's Kinross but more an essay in decorative baronial, like Fraser's. On the other hand, both *châteaux* were still approached via a series of outer defences which remained from the past; Sir Walter Scott mentions the ones at Glamis and decries their removal to make an English park, 'with gravel up to the front door'. Fraser too has its gravel up to the door, even a new door in a different position, and stands today without fore-buildings, other than those turreted *communs* erected by Lord Fraser in the reign of Charles I.

The last private owners of Fraser, who gave it to the National Trust for Scotland and retired to the 'stables', did a peculiar thing: they scraped the old harling off but re-harled only part of the building afterwards, which makes it look decidedly odd, especially in the places they have chosen to leave exposed in 'naked stonework', though there may be 'method in their madness' since the harled parts are the latest bits, and the unharled the oldest. In a rather cryptic comment on Fraser in an article in *Country Life* which appeared shortly after the place had gone to the Trust, the author mentions Fraser's escape from the attention of 'Scotland's most celebrated architect of this century'—a reference no doubt to Sir Robert Lorimer, though its escape from David Bryce, in the nineteenth century, was much more significant. Lorimer's whimsy may be deplored but was never dull, nor did he use standardized plans or materials as Bryce did, and the delightful ogee-topped cupola, with its Renaissance detail around the windows at Fraser, would have delighted the restorer of Balmanno and other baronial homes.

The influence of Fraser seems to have been only slight in the district, and when the Leiths subsequently came to build Leith Hall nearby, in the seventeenth century, they copied only the round towers of Lord Fraser's *communs*, which they added when they created the first part of what was to become a courtyard structure. The family emanated from near Edinburgh, where

Leith Hall, Aberdeenshire

they were merchants in Leith, but they soon established themselves in the Garioch and, until the sad demise of the last heir, at the age of twenty-one in the first months of the 'Phoney War' in 1939, served the neighbourhood as true inheritors of the baronial tradition.

An odd survival of this can be seen in the sycamore tree, the 'furca' from which wrong-doers were hung upside down till they repented. This is almost as odd as when the Irvines, when they built their new manor house onto the old tower, simulated the dais in what would have been the lord's hall by a partition and a step up which repeats itself on the next floor, and in a slight raising of the gable end above that, with separate crow-steps and roof! Whether the 'furca' at Leith Hall was ever used as intended, we do not know; it may have had only symbolic status, as did the raising of the floor and roof at Drum. In any case, the baron's judicial rights in that respect were abolished after the Forty-five rebellion, in which, incidentally, the Leith family played a prominent part. The laird was forced to live abroad after Culloden, and in the house they have one of the very few official Pardons granted, so that he could return and, after fighting against George II, fight for George III.

Leith Hall, like Abergeldie Castle, began life as a simple rectangle, with corner turrets and stair tower, but today, after three transformations, it is nearly square, with a courtyard in the middle, each addition being done with respect for what went before, so that, as previously mentioned, low, conically capped towers '*à la* Fraser' stand at the westernmost corners; turrets were placed on the top storey of the Georgian wing, and more low-level round towers with conical caps adorn the projecting eastern entry, erected at the end of the nineteenth century. This 'porch' emulates work at Fyvie Castle, which a branch of the Leith family acquired at that time.

The renown of Fyvie has almost eclipsed that of the castles of Mar, especially recently when it came up for sale and gained the front page of *The Scotsman*. One is not quite sure why this should be so, as it is a building which has been much altered down the ages and has belonged to a number of families, the Forbes Leiths having acquired it from the Gordons, the Gordons from the Setons, the Setons from the Meldrums, and the Meldrums from the Prestons; before that it was royal, Edward I of England having stayed in an earlier castle. Unlike Drum, or Craigievar or Crathes, or many of the other baronial seats that have gone to the National Trust, Fyvie lacked many ancestral furnishings and boasted no long-established lairds to be dispossessed in any *changement*; the National Trust for Scotland, who now have it, will be obliged not only to look after an L-shaped building roughly two hundred feet by two hundred, and six storeys in height but to maintain it with valuable furniture and *objets d'art*.

The first owners are represented by the Preston Tower, at Fyvie's easternmost end, the Meldrums by one at the westernmost, the Gordons by one at the northern end of the L, and the Setons by the central feature which is the *pièce de résistance* of the entire structure.

Alexander, Lord Fyvie, was educated in Italy and studied law in Paris, whence he returned to Scotland to astonish the youthful James VI and his councillors by his learning, ability and culture. He was made Lord Chancellor and in due course Earl of Dunfermline. He was also put in charge of the education of the King's second son, Charles, the future Martyr King. R. W. Billings, in his book *The Baronial and Ecclesiastical Antiquities of Scotland*, suggests that, since the Earl was a Roman Catholic, that may have inclined Prince Charles in that direction. In fact, Charles I never showed the slightest leanings towards papalism, unless one reads that into a comment he made at the height of his tormenting at the hands of the Covenanters, that he would rather have one pope than a dozen of them! The fact is, he died a martyr's death for the Anglican Church.

However, Charles could very well have gained his first interest in architecture, pictures and sculpture from his gifted Scottish guardian, for the Earl of Dunfermline was a typical and able son of the Renaissance. His centrepiece at Fyvie, in which he joined the two separated eastern and western towers with two smaller ones, themselves joined under a great, high-level arch, was not only remarkably successful but set an example for Bruce himself to follow, when he came to create a suitable frontispiece at Thirlestane for his patron the Duke of Lauderdale. Inside too, the so-called François Premier staircase, with its heraldic décor and arched supports could have been conceived only by a 'master', and that master was the Earl himself. It may not be wide or high enough to be ridden up on horseback, as the one at Amboise is,

Winton House, formerly Wintoun Castle, East Lothian

but very nearly so, and quite as beautiful.

Chancellor Seton also built Pinkie House near Musselburgh, with its rather more English flavour, the ornamental fountain in the courtyard recalling work at Hatfield, and the long gallery, with its colourful cherubs, foliage and classical allusions, the more sophisticated examples found south of the border. Pinkie has some good plasterwork as well, notably in 'the king's room', which is of a slightly later date since it was made for the reception of Charles I when he came to Scotland for his coronation at Holyrood Abbey in 1637, some time after the demise of his erstwhile tutor and mentor. The King did not stay in Edinburgh but travelled up each day with his suite, which was housed partly here, partly in Seton Palace, nearer the coast, and partly at Wintoun (now spelt Winton), seat of George Seton, third Earl of Wintoun, who made his marvellous house largely as we see it today, except for some battlemented additions created in the early nineteenth century by John Paterson, a pupil of Robert Adam and architect of Eglinton Castle, in Ayrshire.

Eglinton, which became a seat of the earls of Seton and

Montgomerie, has since been dynamited more or less out of existence, giving the additions at Winton slightly more importance, but I know both Sir David Ogilvy, the present laird, and his father would willingly have pulled them down. As a matter of fact, the late Gilbert Ogilvie, who was a qualified

Renaissance details at Winton

architect, did mollify the 'Gothycke' effects here and there, by removing battlements and putting back ogee-roofed turrets.

Winton was badly damaged during the 'Rough Wooing', when the Earl of Hertford, on orders from Henry VIII, ravaged the Borders in an attempt to make the Scots agree to the marriage of Mary, Queen of Scots, to his son, the future Edward VI. The Scots replied by sending their Queen to France and resisting the Tudor army sent against them. They lost at the Battle of Pinkie, but Mary was betrothed to the Dauphin François. The old fortalice was not destroyed, only damaged, and it was soon repaired. It was not until the Jacobean era, however, that the present splendid building was created on the same site. It is L-shaped but for the aforementioned battlemented acretions, which are largely one storey in height and mostly around the front door. This has meant the old entry being done away with, the pedimented doorpiece and attendant heraldry having been

The drawing-room (King's room beyond), Winton House

re-erected in the King Charles Room, or library, as a chimney-piece, while other features such as the royal arms of the first King of Great Britain, have been set in the terrace wall on the east side of the house.

The architect of Winton was William Wallace, Master Mason to King James VI and I and employed by him restoring Edinburgh Castle prior to the royal homecoming of 1617. It is not known how or where Wallace go his understanding of the mature English Jacobean style which is dominant here, with its strapwork, balustradings, Renaissance dormers and, above all, superb chimneystalks, which are not only set diagonally but twisted and turned and fretted in the most extravagant and unique manner—unique in Scotland, that is, for they recall, only in stone, the brickwork marvels in the same genre in the south. Inside Wintoun the plasterwork is likewise of a very high standard, greatly superior to that at Glamis, Muchalls and Craigievar, and obviously by a master, not apprentices. Probably it is by the same plasterer who was sent up from York by the King to work in

Innes House, Moray: note chimney stalks

Edinburgh Castle, though one suspects by the time Charles I arrived some other hand was responsible for the appropriate monograms and armorial devices, national, royal and local that appear on the ceiling of the King's room. In the drawing-room, all is Seton crescents and family heraldry, and the royal coat of arms is that of James VI and I.

Winton House was one of the first buildings of note in Scotland to receive a grant from the Historic Buildings Council. Indeed, the Act creating the Council was actually rushed through Parliament in order to save the plaster ceilings there which were in danger of collapse. It has also had more grants since then than any other historic Scottish building, which shows how important it is considered architecturally. Its innovations and cultural superiority might have had more effect on contemporary work had not the Civil War and a renewed outburst of Calvinistic intolerance and tear of beauty burst upon the country.

Yet Innes House, in Morayshire, does reflect the influence of Winton in a very positive way, and that was built during the

Civil War. Perhaps that was possible because of its distance from Edinburgh and the scene of so much bigotry and strife? At any rate, this L-shaped mansion was designed by William Aytoun, who succeeded William Wallace as King's Master Mason and architect of Heriot's Hospital, the Edinburgh source of so much

Leslie 'Castle': compare it with Innes House

detail at Winton. There is not a lot left inside Innes House to recall the mid-seventeenth century, but its square stair tower with galleried parapet and chimneys set diagonally are clearly from that period, and it is set in a semi-formal garden, walled and surrounded by the trees and meadows of an English park.

In its turn Leslie Castle in Aberdeenshire, on the road between Insch and Rhynie, was influenced in its design by Innes House, though it was not begun until after the Restoration. Its somewhat isolated position made it necessary to retain the old form of pepperpot corner turrets and other defensive features, such as iron bars on the windows and shot-holes at ground level covering the entrance, none of which can be found at Innes or Winton. On the other hand, the L-plan is practically identical, and the square stair tower in the re-entrant angle had a scale-and-platt stair and was topped with similar balustrading. Furthermore, Leslie has diagonally placed chimney stalks at every gable end, and no common crow-steps! It was acquired by the Forbes family by marriage and immediately rebuilt in its present form—that is to say, as it will be again when restored, for it has been a ruin for a long time and only recently bought by an architect with the name of Leslie. (He has matriculated arms and is recognized as Baron of Leslie Castle—not of Leslie: the distinction is significant, since the head of the House of Leslie is the Earl of Rothes.) Although it dates from the second half of the seventeenth sentury, Leslie Castle was apparently surrounded by a moat and was entered through its barmkin wall via a fortified gatehouse and over a drawbridge, so perhaps it deserves the name 'castle', though today it stands alone in a field quite near the road and has not much to set it off.

The three best-known Aberdeenshire families are the Forbeses, the Gordons and the Setons, and of these only the first can be said to be local in origin, the others having come up from the south after Bannockburn. They have also gone in for double-barrelled names, which is distinctly frowned upon at the Lyon Court, not only because it muddles the line of descent and, with it, heraldry, but because, once a good name has had a lesser one added to it, it has already become secondary. There might, I suppose, be some excuse for calling someone Seton-Gordon, since as long ago as the early fifteenth century the heiress of the Gordons married into the Setons and, strictly speaking, since then there have been only Setons, or Seton-Gordons, in Aberdeenshire. It would be interesting to know why the offspring of that heiress decided to drop the Seton and take up Gordon only, for, of course, it is the latter that nowadays counts for most and has even given its name to a district. All three families have been staunchly loyal to the royal House, the wanderings of Lord Forbes of Pitsligo are well known in the north. A philosopher of international repute who carried on long disputations with the French Jansenists, he 'came out' in the Forty-five reluctantly, but inevitably in view of his Jacobite leanings. Then for many years after Culloden he lived the life of a hunted man in the houses of fellow lairds who dared to hide him but more often in the bogs of his native Buckie, supported by his own tenants. The Gordons, largely in the guise of earls and marquises of Huntly, 'Cocks of the North', also suffered all sorts of deprivations for the Stuarts, while the Setons rose and fell with the fate of that unlucky House. They were at their height in the days of Chancellor Seton but by the end of the century had already almost disappeared from the scene and today are much less well known than either of the other two.

With Chancellor Seton a number of Aberdeenshire scions of the same name went south to stay with relations, amongst them Alexander Seton of Pitmedden, an estate in the Formartine district. He was brought up at Winton and studied law in Edinburgh, rising to become a judge, or Senator of the College of Justice, and then, shorty after the Restoration, when his father died of wounds gained serving Charles II, he inherited Pitmedden. He was knighted by the King and subsequently made a baronet of Nova Scotia, with the blood of his family who had died for the cause represented in drops on his coat of arms and baronial banner, while he himself is depicted in his own crest, holding the Scottish Saltire. At Winton he would have been familiar not only with the architectural excellencies of the place but with its formal gardens, now gone for ever. These gardens, which were common at the time, were based on Italian precepts as they came to Scotland via France and were laid out in geometrical patterns, either floral or armorial and set within low box hedges, coloured gravel, sand and stones being used with hundreds of potted plants to produce the required effects. There is a splendid bird's-eye view of Edinburgh by James Gordon of Rothiemay done about 1647 which shows such gardens, large and small, behind the houses in the High Street and more particularly at Holyroodhouse.

James Gordon was both minister and laird of Rothiemay, in Banffshire, and the son of Robert Gordon of Straloch, with whom he had helped to complete the set of maps of Scotland which the Reverend Timothy Pont had begun in the reign of James VI and I and which had been continued by Sir John Scot of Scotstarvit but got held up by the Civil War. They were eventually published in Amsterdam by John Blaeu. Straloch was an Aberdeenshire barony; it still is, though no longer appertaining to the Gordons and joined with that of Barra. The house at Straloch is not particularly old, though the one at Barra, which belonged to the Setons is, at least in origin. The castle there was restored during last century but looks most picturesque behind its courtyard, its rude granite towers rising straight from the ground and easily seen from the road, near Old Meldrum, not far from the site where Robert Bruce beat the Comyns and established his own power in the north. The artist Wenceslaus Holler, who visited Scotland in the mid-seventeenth century, says that Rothiemay's gardens are in some cases inaccurate and in others pure invention; no doubt they would have to be unless he was able to visit every house in the street, but surely his view of the formal garden at Holyrood, still retaining its sundial designed by John Mylne, Master Mason to Charles I, must bear some relation to what was actually there? In any event, Alexander Seton must have known this particular example, as well as Winton, he being well in, so to speak, with the political powers of the day, and determined to create something similar for himself at Pitmedden.

The Great Garden at Pitmedden has been re-created by the National Trust for Scotland under the guidance of the late Dr James Richardson, former Chairman of the Royal Commission on Ancient Monuments in Scotland. It is the only one of its kind in the country and a marvellous memorial to Sir Alexander Seton who first laid it out. Like others of his family he lost favour at Court towards the end of the seventeenth century. King James VII and II sent instructions for his name to be struck off the list of judges, no doubt because he opposed that monarch's Jesuitical policies, and he then retired to his Aberdeenshire estate. Bit by bit the huge formal garden, with its gazebos and bath-house, fountains and sundials, became a wilderness and ended its more recent days as a vegetable plot! It was, therefore, something of a challenge to the Trust to try to restore it as it might have been in late Stuart times. There were no plans to go by, only notes and a few surviving items such as the great sundial with its twenty-four facets, each set back concavely from the face, the three walls, or terraces from which the formal patterns could be seen, the outline of the gardens houses and monumental entry steps.

Dr Richardson went straight to Rothiemay and his view of the Caroline gardens at Holyrood. He also associated Alexander Seton with Sir William Bruce, since the dismissed judge certainly would have been well known to Charles II's Architect Royal. Taking the formal layout at Holyrood as a guide, a new layout was devised for Pitmedden, the central feature being Seton's own coat of arms, with the drops of blood around the Seton heart

Hill of Tarvit, Fife, with terrace in style of Bruce

and crescents. The gazebos were restored, the northernmost one given an ogee roof like Bruce's at Kinross, its upper chamber being furnished with cane-seated, high-backed chairs of the period, the bottom restored as a bath-house. The main terrace Richardson decided to relate directly to Bruce's Italian terrace at Balcaskie and in particular to re-create, only in evergreens, the stone buttresses of that terrace. Curiously enough, Sir Robert Lorimer had already set a precedent in this form at Hill of Tarvit, near Ceres, in Fife.

Hill of Tarvit replaced Wemysshall, which before that had replaced the old tower house of Scotstarvit as *caput* of the barony. Wemysshall was traditionally designed by Sir William Bruce and was a modest country house of the late seventeenth century with simple pedimented centrepiece and front door with moulded architraves and, the sure hallmark of Bruce, plain, rusticated quoins (cornerstones). It was bought in the reign of King Edward VII by a Dundee jute merchant who had acquired a fine collection of French furniture and *objets d'art*, too much to house in Wemysshall and which needed adequate displaying. Lorimer

Pitmedden, Aberdeenshire: the Great Garden

was to create a setting for these by demolishing the older house and building Hill of Tarvit, laying out the grounds at the same time.

Sir Robert Lorimer had no taste for classical architecture—he was too romantic for that; indeed, he even refused to study it properly and used it only when absolutely forced to do so. Here, however, he seems to have fallen to his task with interest. He rebuilt the house in what might be termed a Brucian manner, certainly with rusticated quoins and similar windowframes and details, and chimneys, for which Bruce had been famous, as his not only never smoked but were invariably placed towards the centre of the house, never at gable ends, and thus not only served to keep the rooms warm but became true parts of the architecture.

Besides the new house, the garden gave Lorimer an opportunity to copy Bruce's schemes at Balcaskie, which estate marched with Kellie, where the architect had been brought up and which was, therefore, familiar to him. Hence, no doubt, the terrace at Hill of Tarvit, with its steps and balustrades in the Palladian style and more particularly the clever planting of ever-

Sundial, Pitmedden

green 'buttresses' to emulate Bruce's stone ones. Whether Dr Richardson got the idea for something similar at Pitmedden from this example or direct from Balcaskie, one cannot say but I would suspect the latter, for his evergreen buttresses are wider spaced and less flamboyant in scale, more nearly repeating Bruce's. As for the ogee-roofed gazebo and bath-house, this too had to be re-created and is much in the form of others of the period such as the ones at Melville, at Kinross, of course, and Hatton, where they are all that remains of a once magnificent and extraordinarily well-preserved laird's house and formal garden of the 1780s.

Hatton was a seat of the earls of Lauderdale and was built by the third of them, Charles Maitland, brother of the notorious Duke of that name, Charles II's 'Viceroy' in Scotland. It began life as a feudal tower of the Lauder family, no connection with Lauderdale, and so it stayed until the mid-seventeenth century, when Charles Maitland married Bessie Lauder, the heiress, and created the magnificent house and garden that survived intact inside and out until the mid-fifties of this century. Hatton was not designed by Sir William Bruce but it was built by craftsmen engaged by him at Holyroodhouse and paid for by Charles

Maitland, who was Treasurer-Depute of the Kingdom. A number of very clever rearrangements were made in the process of transforming the old feudal tower into a Restoration mansion of some size and grandeur. The original 'keep' remained at the centre, with a galleried top, and in front a new entrance was built at a

The old entrance to Hatton House, Midlothian

slightly lower level on the model of the central entry to Holyrood. On either side gabled end-pieces were half masked by rounded, conically capped corner towers, and the whole was set on a large podium, laid out as a formal garden, with fountains and box hedges, clipped trees and ornamental plantings. Inside there was sumptuous panelling and plaster ceilings, again the work of craftsmen engaged at Holyrood. All this disappeared almost overnight.

Hatton used to be open on special occasions, the garden well known to Edinburgh folk as a place to go to on summer weekends. Then one night there was a mysterious fire which reduced the building to rubble, its wonderful contents to not much more, and the site to a desert. Even before the remains of the big house were cleared away, a bungalow had appeared nearby, piggeries

and cowbyres, and a petrol pump stood near the old front door. The great podium, with the only surviving large formal garden of the Restoration period in Scotland, simply became a farmyard, and all that remains today is a bath-house, replete with bath, the supporting walls and buttresses, and one decorative arched gateway, which tractors only just manage to avoid and which might as well be taken down and removed somewhere else before they drive into it and it goes too.

Royston, or Caroline Park as it is better known, on the northern side of Edinburgh, down by the Firth of Forth, has fared better, at least in respect of the building. It has no garden, is hemmed in by petrol refineries and gasworks and has only recently ceased to be the offices of an ink firm. Admittedly the ink people looked after it well, but the environment was awful and a disgrace. They sold it to save it, and it was bought by the Duke of Buccleuch, whose family had a connection with it in the past, again merely to save it, since no special use has yet been found for it. One of the staff in the Royal Commission on Ancient Monuments thought it might have made a very good, and suitable, office for them, and so it would, but government departments, even those ostensibly concerned with culture, rarely seem to see things in perspective— that is, an historic building that would not have been expensive to buy and 'do up', and large enough to prevent their buying larger, dispersed properties which they have since done, in noisy and otherwise inappropriate districts.

The old estate of Royston once boasted a castle, which was allowed to become a ruin fairly slowly when Viscount Tarbat, perhaps the biggest 'trimmer' of the late Stuart era, did what the Treasurer-Depute had done at Hatton, namely diverted materials and labour from Holyrood to build what is now called Caroline Park. The datestone on its front states that, 'This small cottage, was built for their own comfort and that of their friends by George and Anna, Viscount and Viscountess Tarbat.' After serving under Charles II and James VII and II as Lord-Justice General and Lord Register, Tarbat had to resign the latter position on being accused of falsifying the Minutes of Parliament for private reasons, despite which William of Orange restored him to his post. Claverhouse, 'Bonnie Dundee', described him as

Caroline Park, Granton: detail of entrance

'a great villain', though he was gifted intellectually and was a member of the Royal Society. He switched sides again after the death of William III and ended his political career in the highest office of all, that of Secretary of State. He had bought the barony of Royston in 1683, and his son, Lord Royston, managed to get an Act of Parliament to let him sell it, on the plea of fictitious debts, in 1739. It was then that it went to the Duke of Argyll and Greenwich and became Caroline Park, the name being that of the Duchess and of Queen Caroline. The house then passed from hand to hand and at one time was rented by Lord Cockburn's father, so that the famous preservationist and co-founder of Britain's oldest amenity society was brought up there as a boy.

Cockburn in his *Memorials* has some harsh things to say about his father, who cut down the trees, destroyed the gardens and removed the superb iron gates that had enclosed the park. It was surely his experiences in the house of a philistine parent that made Henry Cockburn so firm a figure on the other side and probably inspired his comment that one never has to have an excuse for cutting a tree down, only for retaining it or planting a new one! Not a gazebo or trace of the formal garden that must have existed here, as it did at Hatton and has recently been re-created at Pitmedden, is to be found, though the gates can still be seen gracing someone else's entrance, on the Glasgow road out of Edinburgh. On them are the arms of Stewart, no doubt those of Sir John Stewart of Allanbank, in Berwickshire, who was a friend of Scott and occupied Caroline Park shortly before the Cockburns came.

The interior of the house too, though unappreciated and unused, survives in the major part, the plaster ceilings and panellings especially, plus a set of splendid wall paintings by de la Cour, who decorated a number of Scottish houses near Edinburgh in the mid-eighteenth century and who concentrated on highly romanticized local scenes. There are also two very fine staircases, one with carved timber balustrades, the other in what must be uniquely rich Baroque ironwork, it being the creation of German craftsmen. In fact, many of the finer details, as opposed to the more general features, are by others than the Holyrood labour force, and later in date. It was Nicolas Heude, for example, who painted the central panel in the large plaster ceiling in the drawing-room. He was a pupil of Verrio, who did so much work

Prestonfield House, Edinburgh (with modern porch)

at Hampton Court for William and Mary, and Queen Anne.

Even further removed from Holyrood is the south front at Caroline Park, which has been attributed to Bruce but cannot possibly be, not only because its late date precludes his active participation but because of the comparative crudeness of its details. After so much sophistication inside the house (the best plaster ceilings were probably the work of itinerant Italians), it is odd to find so bold but only moderately well proportioned a front as this one. Its projecting end pavilions are roofed *à l'impériale*, and the same curvaceous form is simulated over the entrance, but the placing of the windows, the over-heavy rustications and fairly clumsy porch could never have been done by Bruce. The nearest examples of such work, only better designed and executed, are the pavilions at Champ-de-Bataille, in Normandy, a sort of country Vaux-le-Vicomte and probably by a member of the same family. How it came to Scotland one simply does not know; there are no records to guide us, only the possibility that the creator of this strangely foreign front can have visited France at the beginning of the eighteenth century, or could it be an amusing concoction of some gifted master mason, given his head by the ageing Tarbat?

Before we go on to discuss manor houses and smaller mansions by Bruce himself, it may be as well to say something about one more house near Edinburgh which has been attributed to him but which cannot be proved. This is Prestonfield, or Priest Field, which had for lairds the Dick family. Although it is now an hotel, it is run more like a private house and has retained almost all its Restoration décor, including leather hangings, panelling, plaster ceilings and ornate chimneypieces. The Dick of the day, when the papist James, Duke of York, was sent by a somewhat sly Charles II as Lord High Commissioner to the Church of Scotland, was a co-religionist of the Duke and had his house burnt down in an anti-popish student riot. The King's brother made Treasury funds available for its rebuilding and sent workmen from Holyrood to do it. The theory is that Bruce also took part in this. It is true the details are good and he may have guided some master mason's hand. It has a somewhat homely look, with two chimney-capped Dutch gables, linked by a galleried centrepiece, but its proportions are good. The present porch is Georgian, as are some bay windows and additions on the garden side, yet the feel of Prestonfield is of Bruce, at least until one gets inside when the overblown richness of some of the décor lacks his refinement and patrician taste—indeed, it makes one think more of the frilly Nell Gwyn side of Restoration life. At any rate it is of its period and intact. It was visited in the eighteenth century by Bonnie Prince Charlie and by Dr Samuel Johnson and James Boswell.

Originally Prestonfield, or Priest Field, as the name implies, had a religious connotation, but when the monkish owners supported Edward III of England against their own king, David II, they were dispossessed and the property went to the Crown. The reddendo had been a pair of gloves which the holder had to present to his sovereign each St Giles Day. Sir James Dick was a close acquaintance of James, Duke of York, and managed to acquire the barony in 1677, the Duke often walking over from Holyrood, through the park to the other side of Arthur's Seat to visit his co-religionist friend. It was this association, of course, which brought on the riot of 1681. It looks, however, as if some of the present contents were at Sir James Dick's town house at the time and not, therefore, burnt, which may account for the remarkably well-preserved state of such things as the leather hangings, which are known to have been bought in Spain, at

Kinross House from the south showing massed chimney-stalks and, on the left, garden gazebo

Cordoba, in 1676. All trace of any formal garden that may have existed has gone, and the grounds at Prestonfield have been 'landscaped' after the English manner, but at least one touch of exoticism appropriate to the Restoration period is displayed by the peacocks that roam the lawns and make their peculiar cry from the top of walls and hedges.

Having been sent to Scotland by his brother to be out of the way, the future James VII and II periodically returned south uninvited just to see what was going on. He was particularly anxious not to be away when the King died and so, possibly, be passed over for the throne. In fact, it may have been because of this that Bruce designed Kinross House so grandly and expensively. It has no equal north of the border and few south and is clearly too big and splendid for the average red-bonneted laird, which Bruce was, so that the Duke of York could live there if

159

Kinross House: the 'fish gate' and Loch Leven Castle

excluded from Whitehall. This is certainly one explanation which has been given for Kinross, which Bruce never quite finished, having run out of funds, his wife not having enough or good enough clothes to attend the coronation of King James when he finally 'made it'.

Returning from one of his reconnaissance trips to London, the Duke's ship ran aground off Yarmouth, and as the crew made for safety, leaving Duke and nobles to drown, the latter drew their swords and forced a way for James, and his dogs, which were saved. In the course of this exercise a number of Scottish gentlemen were lost, not Sir James Dick, happily, but Charles Hope of Hopetoun, his infant son being subsequently ennobled in his father's stead. It was he who built Hopetoun House, now no manor house but a vast palace. The architect was Sir William Bruce. Had the new Earl of Hopetoun's dilettante nephew, the Marquis of Annandale, not suggested it, the Adam family would not have been engaged, undoing all Bruce's good, refined work and disguising it under a heavy cover of Vanbrughesque display. Hopetoun would then have remained the former Architect

160

Royal's masterpiece, even more gracious and accomplished than Kinross itself.

The Marquis of Annandale had himself employed Bruce at Craigiehall, nearby, but not satisfied with that had himself engaged William Adam there also; the result was partially removed by Sir Robert Lorimer, but unfortunately Craigiehall is now Army Headquarters (Scotland), and, apart from a little panelling and a handsome staircase in wrought iron in the manner of the one at Caroline Park, there is not much to show for late seventeenth- and early eighteenth-century efforts. One thing the Marquis of Annandale did do that was of value, and far reaching in its effect, though he could not have known it at the time, was to encourage the younger members of the Hope family to do the Grand Tour of Europe and to take with them Robert Adam. From this originated almost the whole career and international fame of the brothers Adam.

5. Gentlemen's Houses

When Inigo Jones, returning from Italy after a visit made under the aegis of Queen Anne of Denmark, designed the 'Queen's House' at Greenwich, the effect was immediate and startling. Englishmen had not before seen such a clean, white, perfectly proportioned work of architecture. They were used to half-timbering and red tiles, thatch, brick and some stone, almost all semi-medieval in ethos, though there were some large, rather over-decorated mansions in Tudor and Jacobean style which owed something to Italian models, but which were vulgar in the extreme compared to this new white perfection imported from the Venetian *terra firma* by the Queen's favourite architect; this was a direct importation of Palladianism, undiluted by native adaptation.

Sir William Bruce has been called 'the Inigo Jones of Scotland' in that he too imported a Continental style of architecture neat, though he was more of an age with Christopher Wren, being born in 1630, the same year as Charles II, and dying in 1710, in the reign of Queen Anne. He was of royal descent and proud of it, and as a young man went to Holland to meet the exiled King and start negotiations for his return to his throne in 1660. He was rewarded with the post of Clerk to the Bills, which meant he collected a fee on every Bill that went through the Scottish Parliament, and was created a baronet of Nova Scotia. Through his cousin Bessie Lauderdale, scheming duchess of the King's 'Viceroy', he obtained the job of enlarging Thirlestane Castle, the Lauderdales' Border seat, and thence never looked back until Holyrood was completed for the arrival of James, Duke of York, some years later.

Bruce's own first house, at Balcaskie, in Fife, is sometimes reckoned the first mansion-house in Scotland. There he adapted and enlarged an old laird's tower and experimented externally and internally until he went to Kinross in the 1680s, having planted the park and garden there well in advance. Most of his commissions came through relations and close personal contacts: Holyrood, of course, through the Lauderdales, and Moncreiffe House followed his purchase of Balcaskie from the Moncreiffe of that Ilk, while Dunkeld came through a cousin by marriage. Both these houses were what is called 'double pile'—that is, two rooms thick, with a central hall, and entry on either side, the rooms being symmetrically disposed to left and right, with a separate place at one end for the stairs. At Kinross Bruce managed pages' quarters on a mezzanine floor and made the vista, which began a quarter of a mile away at the entrance gates, stretch right through the front door to the garden side, and on out to a view of Loch Leven Castle on its island in the middle of the Loch. The avenues and plantings generally recall scenes in the Ile de France, and the whole conception came from over the Channel.

Moncreiffe was similar, only on a smaller scale, but had no loch or castle to take into the view between the forest *allées*, though Balcaskie has the Bass Rock, which can be seen clearly from the central windows of the house right across the Firth of Forth.

Many of Bruce's houses were quite modest, and always he retained more ancient remnants wherever possible. In this he differed absolutely from most Palladian architects and showed his native love of tradition, his Scottishness, if you like. The stable block at Kinross is a perfect example of this. In his gardening too there were interesting variations and occasional hark-backs, but that formal parterre at Holyrood which Dr Richardson copied at Pitmedden was before his time and already out of date in its layout before ever Bruce came to work at the palace. It survives in modified form still, in the Queen's private garden and at least retains an old sundial at its centre designed by John Mylne, father of the master mason employed by Bruce, on which are the monograms of Charles I, Henrietta Maria and Charles, Prince of Wales.

Though he was a Stuart supporter, Bruce never got on with James, Duke of York (few people did), and after the arrival of William of Orange he retired to Kinross. Curiously enough, however, he still received many commissions, including a number from members of the new Whig establishment. Hopetoun was perhaps the most important, and another rather unusual task was the marriage column of James, fourth Earl of

Panmure, and Margaret, daughter of the third Duke of Hamilton, which he designed and which was erected in 1693, when Jacobitism was at its lowest ebb. The old house of Panmure, near Dundee, was built by Robert Mylne, the same who worked with Bruce at Holyrood, and, in common with Craighall, Hatton and

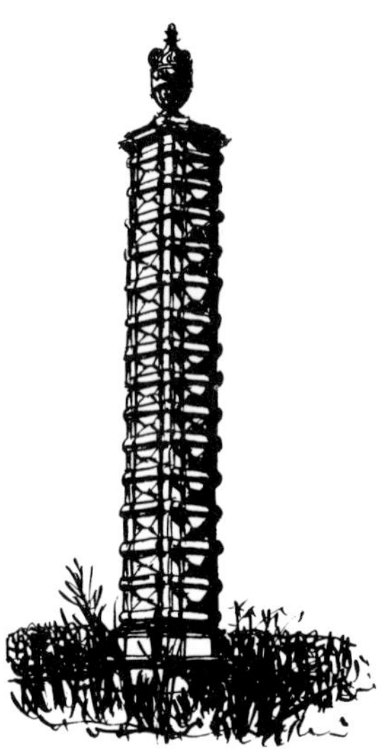

Marriage Column, Panmure, Angus

several other buildings of the period, has since disappeared, blown up in the 1950s. The Panmures, now joined with the Ramsay family, went to live at Brechin Castle, which I will describe in another context, but standing isolated and rather lonely, in the midst of a pine forest, their marriage column survives for those who care to seek it out, plus some old gates and walls that once were Panmure itself.

Sir William Bruce married twice (some have said thrice but where they get that from I can't imagine), and his widow survived him late into the eighteenth century, actually befriending Flora MacDonald and others involved in the Forty-five rebellion. She was a Scott of Galashiels, and this may account for Bruce's being asked to design Harden House, now known as

Mertoun, for his relatives by marriage the Scotts of Harden.

Harden is the best of Bruce's houses after Kinross, of which it is a smaller version, and appears in William Adam's *Vitruvius Scoticus* with two elevations and plans. The date of erection was 1703, as a datestone recently found in one of the garden gazebos

Bruce's garden elevation for Harden (Mertoun), Berwickshire

proves, and on the front are the arms and crest of the Scotts of Harden. Later in its history Harden became the property of the Bridgewaters, and the Duke famous for covering England with canals enlarged and obliterated the old house without actually pulling it down. He needed somewhere to hang the Orleans Collection which he had bought after the French Revolution and which included two sumptuous Titians which Charles I would have got in his dowry if he had married the Infanta and not frittered away his time in Madrid with the Duke of Buckingham. These pictures and others remained on the walls of a greatly enlarged Harden, or Mertoun, until after the last war, the house being requisitioned by the Scottish National Galleries as a place of safety for art treasure.

Auchindinny House, Midlothian

It was some time later that the Duke of Sutherland, or Lord Ellesmere as he then was, obtained permission to remove the additions and get back to Bruce's original house. He sent the larger and more valuable pictures on semi-permanent loan to the National Gallery in Edinburgh and proceeded, with Ian Lindsay's expert help, to uncover what was left of Harden from beneath its outer casing of uncomplimentary nineteenth-century masonry. When the work was completed, there was the house very much as it appears in *Vitruvius Scoticus*, except that Bruce's nicely placed chimney stalks had gone, replaced by larger ones and at the gable ends, and one or two minor details, such as the datestone, had been removed (but it was recovered). Inside, unhappily, nothing remained as designed. It was a new house, but remarkable that after all so much of the fabric was intact, including the two end pavilions without which no Bruce house could be said to be complete, and linking low walls. There used to be a small hamlet by the name of Mertoun; hence the nomenclature that replaced Harden when the property changed hands, and in the grounds, which are very beautiful, the house standing near a lovely bend of the River Tweed amidst fine woods and

Mertoun's old doocot

policies, are the original kirk, old Mertoun House, which dates from Jacobean times, and an interesting contemporary doocot.

It is arguable that Auchindinny House, between Edinburgh and Penicuik, is the most attractive of all Bruce designs. It is certainly his smallest and in the event the last, since his very last, Nairne House in Perthshire, was maliciously demolished by the Hanoverian Duke of Atholl in order to make 'a Carthage' of the Nairne property, they, his cousins, being avid Jacobites and Tories. One sees Auchindinny nicely from the road, where the architect dictated there should be a vista from the house towards some outstanding natural object, in this case Castle Law, in the Pentland Hills. The building is that rare thing in Scotland a genuine Queen Anne house. There are so many in England, but southerners should remember that the Augustan reign of 'Great Anna whom three realms obey' was not the same north of the Border. The Act of Union of 1707 was not welcomed by all and was accompanied by riots and disorder, plot and counter-plot, the whole lot rife with misunderstandings and misrepresentations, some of the mythology of which still clings. The serenity of Auchindinny, which in its present form, except for three rather prominent dormer windows which date from the Georgian era, belongs to the first decade of the eighteenth century, is not typical of Scotland at that time. Even Bruce himself was suspect, being a supporter of the old line of Kings; he was locked up more than once for failing to appear at official functions which would have been embarrassing to him.

Bruce's House stands on the foundations of a 'Toure and Manor place' of 1557, the vaulted lower, or laich, hall obviously surviving from then, as, possibly, does a small spiral stair in one of the side pavilions. As it stands today, however, Auchindinny is completely of its period and typical of its architect, the perfect symmetry of the main front, the steps rising to a pedimented front door, the 'lugged' (eared) window surrounds on the side pavilions, the simple margins to emphasize corners, and the low semi-circular curtain walls, which are miniature versions of those at Kinross and elsewhere. The stone is a pleasant reddish shade, Mertoun's is dove-grey, and the immediate surroundings are charming to a degree. It has stayed in the Inglis family and their descendants ever since it was built, though tenanted in the late eighteenth and early nineteenth century by Henry Mackenzie,

Gallery House, Angus, *c*.1680

Scott's particular friend and author of *The Man of Feeling*. His *Anecdotes and Egotisms* are a valuable and interesting record of his times, from the days of Jacobitism to those of George IV, which was the most memorable from a cultural point of view in the history of Edinburgh, the 'Golden Age' of the 'Athens of the North'. In his *Anecdotes* Mackenzie refers to Auchindinny, to its design by Bruce and to the fact that his chimneys never smoked. Much of the interior of the house has survived, a good deal of panelling, the Memel pine attractively done out in pale blue-green, as it should be, and one unpainted room in oak. Upstairs there are a number of de la Cour's romantic perspectives, while in the dining-room two old windows with thick astragals still contain their early eighteenth-century hand-flung glass.

Inland from Montrose and just north of Brechin is the House of Gallery. It is not by Bruce, nor is any other particular name associated with it, but its site, in the depths of rural Angus, and its design make it unique. The barony was that of the Foulertons, or Fullertons, fowlers to the king, and the house, which dates from the second half of the seventeenth century, is quite remark-

169

able for its symmetry and poise, its excellent heraldry and fine contemporary plaster ceilings. In the upper drawing-room, for instance, amongst the more usual swags, are fowls, pigeons anyway, while similar versions representative of the family's official function appear on top of the gateposts of the walled garden. The main building is foursquare and uncompromising but well proportioned and good, of three storeys and high-pitched roof such as one might find in one of the remoter provinces of France, Auvergne perhaps, which makes one sorry we did not have a more peaceful and prosperous history here in Scotland, otherwise this is the kind of decent country architecture we would have had and which would have given us a native style that owed nothing to lairds' towers and bad-tempered defensive edifices.

Gallery is large, three-storeyed and completely domestic and settled looking. Over the front door is Fullerton heraldry, and on either side two projecting wings are capped almost exactly as those at Balcaskie, though the walls are harled and not exposed stone as in Bruce's house. The finials are dated 1680. Behind are magnificent barns and other buildings symptomatic of a plenitude that one rarely associates with Scotland, but which is there just the same, especially in Angus and Kincardineshire, which are far enough away from both Highlanders and southern marauders to prosper if left to go their own ways and not be for ever dragged into other people's politics.

There were three waves of plasterers in Scotland during the seventeenth century, the first when James VI and I returned home in 1617, the second attendant upon Charles I's coronation at Holyrood in 1633, and the third following Bruce's restoration of Holyroodhouse for Charles II. The latter seem to have got pretty far afield as well, not the original craftsmen but certainly men trained in the same tradition as the King's 'gentlemen modellers' from Windsor, who came north expressly at royal command. The 'Merry Monarch' had no desire to revisit his northern kingdom especially after the way he had been treated there in 1650-51, but, just in case he was obliged to, he made sure that Holyroodhouse was rendered as elegant and comfortable as possible; that is why so many really excellent artists were sent up to work there, and this set standards in other parts of the country which might never have been the case, or would certainly have been greatly delayed

Newhailes, Midlothian

in their effect. So the plasterers, who worked at Balcaskie for Bruce when they were not too busy at Holyrood, sent apprentices north, to Gallery, as we have seen, to Arbuthnott, in Kincardine-shire, to Fyvie and beyond, to Brodie, near Nairn, which is the furthest north they got.

Sir William Bruce had one clear successor, not only as Surveyor to the King but as principal architect in the kingdom, in James Smith. The first post he acquired from James VII and II, partly no doubt since he was a fellow papalist, but Smith succeeded in retaining his position after the fall of the last Stuart and into the reign of Queen Anne. He was unimaginative but well trained, understood perspective and put his chimney stalks in the right place. In fact, he is now known to have been the draughtsman of many of Colin Campbell's collection in the Royal Institute of British Architects and has, therefore, a much more important place in the history of the spread of Palladianism in Britain as a whole than is generally thought. He designed the kirk of the Canongate for King James, when that monarch threw out the congregation from the chapel at Holyrood to make it into a combined Roman Catholic place of worship and seat of the Order of the Thistle, which order he instituted in the form it has since come down to us.

James Smith was married to Janet Mylne, daughter of the Master Mason to the King in Scotland who, with Bruce, rebuilt the Palace of Holyroodhouse. He is said to have had thirty-two children, and lived between 1646 and 1730. He bought the estate of Whitehill, near Inveresk, in Midlothian, and built there the house which is now known as Newhailes, it having become the seat in Georgian times of the judge Lord Hailes, who himself enlarged it with the aid of William Adam. Smith was 'of Whitehill' and received from the Lyon King a grant of arms, 'azure three falmes of fire, or; on a chief argent, a thistle, vert'. He did some work at Traquair, including the design of two charming ogee-roofed pavilions in the matter of those at Melville, and produced a scheme, not done, for making the whole front symmetrical. In other respects he followed the example of Sir William Bruce, and most importantly he began Yester House for the Marquis of Tweeddale. The Marquis was a great anglophile and connoisseur of trees and shrubs and, besides wishing to create a handsome new mansion in place of his erstwhile medieval castle, sought actually to copy the royal parks at Greenwich and St James in London. His son married the daughter of the Duke of Lauderdale, became Lord Chancellor under Queen Anne and that Queen's High Commissioner to the Scottish Parliament in the days immediately preceding the Union of 1707, of which he was a keen supporter.

The old castle of Yester, now reduced to its dungeons and subterranean vaulted passages and nicknamed 'Goblin's Ha', was the creation, in the first place, of the Norman family of de Giffard, one of whom was Gonfalconier to William the Conqueror and whose earlier seat, the motte at Longueville, is in Normandy. The branch of the family which settled at Yester subsequently married into the de Hayes, or Hays, they being named after the high hedges, or haies, of Normandy; they have been at Yester ever since, at least until shortly after the death of the eleventh Marquis of Tweeddale and the departure south of his second wife. It is now the home of the Italian opera-composer Giancarlo Menotti.

A little beyond our scope as a typical manor on account of its size, though it is not a palace like Hopetoun, Yester is interesting in that it was begun by James Smith and Alexander MacGill, who based it on a scheme of Bruce, and was completed at the time of the French Revolution and the death of Robert Adam, who contributed, amongst other things, a most delightful small study upstairs in perfect neo-classical style. Inside Yester the whole Adam family worked, as at Hopetoun, James and Robert taking over where their father left off, completing one of the finest series of rooms in Roman Baroque in the country. These rooms are also decorated by William de la Cour, who was Director of the Academy of Fine Arts in Edinburgh and whose panels at Caroline Park we have noted. The house is some way from 'Goblin's Ha', and the main lodge opens at right angles to the village street, with its 'new' whitewashed kirk and pub and douce Scotch houses of the early eighteenth century, the whole being the special creation of the second Marquis who first slept in his grand but unfinished manor house in about 1702.

Bruce drew plans for Melville House in Fife for the Earl of Leven and Melville but, as in several other cases, Smith carried them out and adapted them to the exigencies of the site. A particularly interesting example of this was at Raith, also in Fife, but facing the Firth of Forth on a high hill behind Kirkcaldy. Lord Raith was the Earl of Leven and Melville's son and an important figure in early eighteenth-century Scottish politics, being Treasurer-Depute in succession to the Duke of Lauderdale's brother, Lord Hatton, subsequent third Earl of Lauderdale. The house he commissioned must have been one of the best of its period and, being smaller than Melville or Yester, even Kinross, must have exuded a charm few others, except perhaps Mertoun and Auchindinny, did.

Like Melville and Mertoun, Raith had a central cupola, since gone, boasted the usual well-placed chimneys, had low curved side walls ending in pavilions and was entered by a *perron* through a typically pillared doorway. In the tympanum of the central gable were the arms of the lord and lady of the manor, in this case Lord Raith and his wife, Barbara Dundas, but these have been removed by a later owner, the Treasurer-Depute having no heir. Later owners also raised the curved side wings by a storey, completely altering the scale of these adjuncts in relation to the house itself, and further destroyed the architectural balance by demolishing the original end pavilions and replacing them with houses big enough to be in competition with the modest mansion at the centre. Inside almost everything of value has gone save a

Airds House, Argyll

delightful iron back stair decorated with a baron's coronet above the letter R, and a few pieces of plasterwork.

The influence of building such as Raith must have been quite considerable at the time and gone on being so well into the eighteenth century. At Airds, for instance, is a house that might almost have been designed by Sir William Bruce himself, so charming is it, so beautifully poised and symmetrical, almost perfect in its design and setting, yet dating from about 1738. More surprising even than the date is its setting and how it got there, for Airds is on the west coast of Argyll, in Appin, which is traditionally Stewart country, and contended for down the ages by the Campbells. It was a Campbell who built Airds, after vacating Castle Stalker, the ancient redoubt of the Stewarts of Appin and hunting lodge of James IV. The Stewarts held the castle for the King but that did not stop the Campbells periodically driving them out and ravaging their lands; indeed, the whole history of the place shows how slight a hold, if any, the kings of Scots maintained in these parts. The Campbells of Airds were descended from the illegitimate son of a Campbell of Calder

(Cawdor) who married an illegitimate daughter of the sixth Earl of Argyll, and they were confirmed in their possessions, really those of the Stewarts of Appin, by the notorious Marquis of Argyll in 1643. The King never recognized any such confirmation, and at the Restoration the Stewarts appealed to the Privy Council to get their property back. They won their case but Dingwall Pursuivant, who was sent by the Lord Lyon to execute the Council's orders, was beaten up by the Campbell's had his herald's trumpet bent and was told to go back whence he came. So much for the royal authority.

The Stewarts of Appin did, subsequently, regain their inheritance for a few years until the flight of James VII and II, when they fought under 'Bonnie Dundee' at Killicrankie. Castle Stalker was finally surrendered to the Campbells in 1690, and the family of Airds stayed there until moving to their new Palladian house. Donald Campbell of Airds, whose arms appear in the pediment, was factor to the third Duke of Argyll but curiously enough seems to have received a letter from Prince Charles Edward appealing for support. He was a captain in the Argyll Militia and actually served under 'Butcher Cumberland', being complimented by his general, the future fourth Duke of Argyll, on his conduct. The General took up residence at Airds with his cousin, and it is pleasant to read that he also tried to calm down the anti-Jacobite reprisals that followed Culloden. Donald, his captain, seems not to have employed any architect on this splendid house, set in what must have been then little more than a wilderness and so far away from everywhere that all the building materials had to come by sea from Glasgow. It was probably the quickest and easiest way, and almost as good as coming by road nowadays over the most tortuous twists and bends, loch heads, mountains and double turns.

One arrives above Airds in its quasi-tropical bay, with luxuriant vegetation falling right down to the sea's edge and a view opening out to myriads of islands stretching to infinity. One must not exaggerate or ignore that fact that it rains for three-quarters of the year in Argyll (hence, at least, the vegetation), but on a clear day, with that translucent light they get in the west, the effect is more than astonishing: it is ravishing. Airds is all white and classical, something Italian in a setting almost Italian in itself. If one is not quite on the road from Santa Margherita to Portofino,

Glendoik, Perthshire

house and scenery are certainly complementary. Here something with an Italian origin fits so marvellously into its blue bay, amidst islands and green hills, that one is tempted to say it has come home.

Not a lot of original fittings exist inside this house at Airds, with its unaltered curtain wings and nice little pavilions. Since it was meant to face the sea and not the land, whoever built it did not bother overmuch what it looked like on the other side, which is now the main entrance. Everything is in proportion, however, the diminishing window sizes on each of the three storeys, the handsome main door and its slightly less important but decorated window over the typical Bruce quoins, and one very special thing: on either side of the projecting centrepiece are eighteenth-century versions of shut-holes, small glazed openings letting in air onto tiny spiral staircases, a return, surely, to the laird's towers of the century before? The barony of Airds is no longer either a Stewart or a Campbell one, and the house, the property of a businessman from Edinburgh, is well looked after and appreciated for its beauty and setting.

Airds has been associated with another attractive white, Palladian house of similarly modest proportions but in Perthshire, Glendoik, which, however, lacks Aird's setting and general poise, though it has its own charm and reminds one a little of the old design for Wemysshall now replaced by Lorimer's Hill of Tarvit. This was Murray country, and in the immediate neighbourhood lived Lord George Murray, Bonnie Prince Charlie's Lieutenant-General, the one who forced the issue at Derby and made the Jacobite troops turn round just at the moment when, hindsight suggests, they might have carried on and taken London. In any event, Glendoik has its associations with Lord George Murray and with the Jacobite cause as such, for it was the seat of Robert Craigie, controversial Lord Advocate and Member of Parliament at Westminster for Dornoch, in Sutherland. Accused of being corrupt and too fond of brandy and claret, he seems to have managed to keep in with Whig and Tory in particularly difficult times whilst personally favouring the Jacobites. He was prominent in the work of the Fisheries Board, had an unrivalled knowledge of the intricacies of feudal law and understanding of the clans and was made Lord President of the Council in 1754. Lord Glendoik died six years later and was buried with the famous in Greyfriars kirkyard in Edinburgh. A child's notebook found amongst his possessions contained the words: 'God save King James and all his family. James the Good and Great, bless him and restore him.'

The house of Glendoik has been connected with the work of William Adam, but it is much more in the manner of earlier buildings, such as Airds, and the later works of Smith and Bruce, not nearly heavy enough for 'Old stone and lime', as the elder Adam was called. When he was inspired, he ladled the swags and urns and columns on with abandon and when not was plain dull. Glendoik is one of the few houses of its kind and period to have retained most of its interior décor and fittings, scale-and-platt mahogany stairs with 'barley-sugar' balusters, nice contemporary panelling and fine plasterwork, with coved ceilings, some of the latter showing shell motif which suggests the work of Thomas Clayton who was employed by William Adam at Hopetoun.

William Adam is said to have been apprenticed to Sir William Bruce but if so he was very young even for those days, and more

Former stable block, Penicuik House, Midlothian

probably this idea emanates from the inclusion in his *Vitruvius Scoticus* of many Bruce houses, starting with Holyrood itself, where Adam worked in the eighteenth century. In fact, the mentor and patron of the elder Adam was Sir John Clerk, second baronet of Penicuik, sometimes called 'the Scottish Lord Burlington'. Sir John's ancestry is interesting as his grandfather was a very early collector of antiques and *objets d'art*, in Paris, who returned to Scotland in the midst of the Civil War troubles and purchased the baronies of Lasswade and Penicuik. The first Sir John was MP for Edinburgh and was made a baronet of Nova Scotia by Charles II. He sent his son to Leyden in Holland to study law, little dreaming what would transpire, for the teen-aged student more or less 'thumbed a lift' over the Alps to Italy where he spent a year enjoying himself in the company of cardinals, princes, musicians, sculptors, painters and architects, acquiring a taste for art beyond his pocket and learning to per-form music 'better than became a gentleman'. He made his way home via Paris, learning to dance there, and for the rest of his life stayed in Scotland except for periodic sorties into England to visit his artistic friends there, including Lord Burlington, and explore archaeological sites of which he was a connoisseur. At home he saved Rosslyn Chapel from complete decay and did much to draw attention to the importance of the Roman Wall between Newcastle and Carlisle; as the Carron Ironworks spread towards the Antonine Wall, he sought to have preserved an amusing

Doocot (Arthur's O'en), Penicuik House

domed object there, which may have been a Roman temple or memorial. Failing in that, he had it copied and erected on the estate at Penicuik. It now fills the eastern side of the courtyard of the stable block, in opposition to a Gibbsian spire he designed, reputedly for the local kirk, but on its being rejected by the Kirk Session he put it here.

Sir John also designed a splendid Palladian mansion to replace his father's and grandfather's manorial pile, but this was not built until after his demise and was then slowly consumed by fire at the end of the nineteenth century. The contents, including the second Sir John's drawings, were saved, and there exist photos of the family and servants sitting outside on the drive watching the smouldering mansion from which they have rescued virtually everything. The present Sir John's grandmother was an artistic person and an Italophile and had the clever idea of converting the stables for a new dwelling and not rebuilding the larger mansion, so that today the Clerks live in the modest but very pleasant manor house she created, entering under the Gibbsian spire into a Florentine-inspired courtyard replete with attractive fountain in the centre and 'Arthur's O'en', as the domed feature is called, serving as doocot on the far side. On it are the words: 'That fair

Mavisbank, Midlothian

dome where suit is paid, by blast of bugle free', a reference, made by Sir Walter Scott, to the Clerks' motto.

The association between Sir John Clerk of Penicuik and William Adam really began when the former employed the latter as his mason on a new mansion he had designed and which he was to call Mavisbank. It was not unlike the Mauritshuis at the Hague, in its central part and Baroque details, and had curtain walls *à la* Bruce and side wings; in order further to educate his mason, i.e. protégé, the baronet took William Adam into England on one of his trips and showed him Castle Howard and other Vanbrugh exercises in architectural theatricality. The effect was not lost on the pupil, alas, since he had neither Vanbrugh's imagination nor skill, and all over Scotland there are examples of the heavier-handed Adam's handiwork in imitative Vanbrughesque. Hopetoun is the largest of these, but the most successful is Duff House, at Banff, which he built but never finished for the

The Drum, Gilmerton, Midlothian

Earl of Fife and which, despite its elaborately contrived façades, rich sculpture, regimented pediments and domed corner towers, is really only an old laird's tower camouflaged, at least as far as its plan is concerned.

Most of William Adam's clients were of the Whig ascendancy, as, indeed, Sir John Clerk was, he being an MP, like his father, and a Commissioner for the Act of Union and Baron of the Exchequer. The latter post was subsequently wound up, but the 'Old Baron' was instrumental in seeing that the 'Equivalent', the amount paid to Scotland by England to make up for the difference in the National Debt, was wisely spent, founding what is now the Royal Scottish Academy and the Fisheries Department and settling Flemish weavers in Picardy Place, Edinburgh. A contemporary of Sir John's was Lord President Robert Dundas, from whom William Adam got the commission to rebuild Arniston, near Lasswade. This was to be a new Palladian house but incorporating the original baronial 'keep', which Adam managed quite successfully, so much so that externally no 'keep' is seen. Inside it is retained in an open hall, elaborately decorated by the Dutch plasterer Joseph Enzer, who worked with Samuel Calderwood and Thomas Clayton at The Drum, Gilmerton, nearer Edinburgh, where Adam next went.

The Drum was begun in the seventeenth century by Lord Somerville, whose hereditary property was at Carnwarth, in Lanarkshire, where his Norman ancestor had slain 'a great worm', no doubt a dragon. His part of The Drum consisted of the three-storeyed wing to the west of Adam's new mansion, which was intended to be repeated on the eastern side. Free from the restraints of Sir John Clerk at Mavisbank, and some that continued whilst employed at Arniston, William Adam launched forth on this over-rusticated but not undistinguished house with gusto. Its glory, however, is in the interior, which is even richer than the exterior but better. The dining-room was done whilst Adam was engaged at Holyroodhouse, and the plasterer was probably Calderwood. Its most interesting feature is a colonnaded recreation of what in a medieval hall would have been called 'the screens', and its most interesting historical connection is when, in 1745, the Jacobites, having entered Edinburgh in triumph, sent out scouts looking for billets and came to The Drum, when the Somervilles threw all the silver out of the dining-room windows into the shrubberies below and so saved some of their possessions.

Of quite a different character are the 'umbrella stands' and triumphs in the hall, very Dutch and overblown and surely by the same Enzer who came from Arniston—at least an article in *Country Life* said so, and so I thought until I went to The Drum and met the late Hamilton More Nisbet on the steps, only to be informed that it was Italians who did the plasterwork and that he had the bills. Then upstairs in the drawing-room the plasterwork is more refined and was probably created by Thomas Clayton. It would certainly be interesting to know who is right, the architect owner of The Drum or visiting experts. It contains more fine plasterwork of the first half of the eighteenth century than any other house of comparable size, and its exterior, though overladen, does recall the Venetian *terra firma* a little, as much as William Adam, who never got further than Belgium in his foreign tours, could conjure up. In front of the house went the old Mercat Cross of Edinburgh when it was proposed to demolish it to make room for the traffic, this was before the days of motor cars. According to Sir Walter Scott, the real reason the magistrates wished it removed was because from it the Old Pretender had been proclaimed in 1745. Anyway it went to The Drum and there stayed safe and sound until Gladstone, MP for Midlothian and Prime Minister, had the good sense to have it returned to its accustomed position in the heart of Edinburgh, under the shadow of the crown spire of St Giles'.

The House of Gray, on the outskirts of Dundee, is falling down

Gray House, Dundee

and emptied of its shutters and chimneypieces and much in need of a helping hand to save it before it is too late. It has all the appearance of a William Adam house but is not Vanbrughesque, more Gibbsian, so may have resulted from another trip south, further south this time, on the part of 'Old Stone and Lime' or possibly have been built while he was still under the influence of Sir John Clerk. In any event, Gray is a handsome building and seems to incorporate the best of Bruce and a burgeoning-better Adam which never burgeoned quite the same again.

The Grays were an old East Lothian family which came to Angus in the fifteenth century and earned a reputation for treachery and cruelty, intrigue and general chicanery on a scale rarely found even in pre-Union Scotland. Their principal seat was Castle Huntly, down by the River Tay, but they also lived at Fowlis Easter, only a few miles from Gray House, which they

Pollok House Glasgow, seen reflected
through bridge

built in 1715. The most notorious of the clan seems to have been
the Master of Gray at the time of Mary, Queen of Scots, and
James VI and I, though his main plan appears not to have been to
murder anyone, at least not unless compelled to, but to try to
produce a peaceful *modus vivendi* between Scotland and England,
Roman Catholic and Protestant, Elizabeth and her cousin, and to
achieve this by a more or less continuously playing off one side
against another. He was certainly a spy in modern terms, a
double-agent, carried secret messages and was prepared to be
ruthless.

Heavy and plain by comparison, both architecturally and
historically, is Pollok House, near Glasgow, *caput* of the Maxwell
barony of that name and, until it was given to the city as a
museum, and its park became the site of the celebrated Burrell
Collection, the home of the late Sir John Stirling Maxwell. He was
a founder member of the National Trust for Scotland, one of the
first Royal Commissioners for Ancient Monuments in Scotland,
and himself gave the first historical building to the nation in the
form of Crookston Castle, on his estate. This was the redoubt of
the Stewarts of Darnley and had for châtelaine in the eighteenth
century an aged and contrite Duchess of Portsmouth, erstwhile

Dumfries House (Terringean Castle): old doocot

mistress of the 'Merry Monarch'. Sir John also was the first important and authoritative person to point to the dangers awaiting Scotland's cultural heritage unless the Scots paid more heed to it and stopped it being destroyed piecemeal. This he highlighted in his *Shrines and Homes* which came out before the war but has since been re-issued. He and his father were considerable collectors of paintings and sculpture, his father especially having one of the finest collections of Spanish paintings in Britain, so that Pollok is undoubtedly the right place for the Burrell Collection to neighbour. The Maxwells were amongst the Saxons who came north with the Normans in the days of David I and already had acquired the barony of Nether Pollok by the thirteenth century. They remained in possession until 1956, when Sir John Stirling Maxwell died there in his ninetieth year. He had no son, otherwise surely it would have continued theirs till today.

Pollok House was designed by William Adam but completed posthumously. It really is plain and a little lumpish and must have been more so until Sir Rowand Anderson was employed by Sir John Stirling Maxwell to soften it up, add side pavilions and surround it with a formal garden. It is now a pleasant place to visit

Auchinleck House, Ayrshire

on a Sunday afternoon, its park a remarkable oasis in the midst of Glasgow's suburbs, the River Cart, which flows through it, a little dirty but not too much so and improved by a weir and a mill that actually works. There is a handsome Palladian bridge over the river as well.

With Pollok we come almost to the end of the influence of William Adam and to that of his sons, or very nearly so, for at Dumfries House, south of the city, we have a gentleman's mansion designed by John and Robert but still with their father in the background. They have not yet evolved a style of their own. As with so many houses in Scotland this one stands on an older estate, and the title has moved from one family to another. The present owner is the Marquis of Bute, Chairman of the National Trust for Scotland, but the land was that of the Crichtons, earls of Dumfries, hence the name, whose house was not a house but a castle of which but one small souvenir remains hale, a beautiful doocot dated 1671 with the laird's coat of arms over the door.

The present Dumfries House was designed by the Adams for the fourth Earl of Dumfries, and no doubt that is what led them to nearby Auchinleck and to build a mansion for the father of the

Scotstoun, *c*.1750

famous diarist, a Law Lord and descendant of the first Boswell to come here from Fife in the early sixteenth century. The name incidentally is pronounced 'Affleck', and that is precisely how the Boswell Tower of Defence north-east of Dundee is spelt. The Place of Auchinleck closely follows, in the design of its central frontispiece, William Adam's main elevation for Elie House shown in *Vitruvius Scoticus* but never carried out. There are differences, of course, and notably in the sculptural details in the tympanum, where one sees scales, caduceus, mace and crown on one side and sword, fasces, trumpet, mace and crown again on the other, all to denote the owner's legal associations. The house is now empty but maintained, belonging to the Boswell Society, who also have an interest in the nearby kirk where Lord Auchinleck added a family vault. The date was 1754, and as William Adam had died, the two amusing Italianate towers at either side of the house must have been by the Adam brothers. The house itself looks home-made by comparison, and may be.

It is interesting how far and wide the various plasterers who came to Scotland, or were already working there, ranged, for throughout the eighteenth century and all over the country one

Scotstoun, Peeblesshire: stable block

comes across quite moderately sized lairds' houses graced inside with perfectly sumptuous ceilings. Such a case is Scotstoun, in Peeblesshire, just beyond Blyth Bridge on the way to Moffat. It is a secretive place, unseen from the road yet set on a slight rise, a sort of podium, in the midst of marshy country, obviously a strong point, though the house as it stands dates only from about 1730. In fact, the Scotts of Buccleuch did have a tower here, probably of wood later rebuilt in stone. What we see today, however, is an attractive long manor house, harled, with stone margins, a nice hipped, or bellcast roof in the Bruce manner, small pedimented centrepiece and pillared porch. Nothing prepares one for the glories within, the well-preserved Baroque ceilings which almost certainly were the creation of itinerant Italians who came to Scotland with all their tools, descended on a house, lived in and on it, then departed, having done their work. Scotstoun was the seat of the Lanarkshire laird Alexander Telfer of Symington when he married Jean Smollett, sister of the renowned historian and novelist, the man who first made *Don Quixote* available to English readers. He visited the house in 1755, when his mother was staying there. It is to this period that the very nice stable block belongs, with its cupola wanting a bell!

On the whole it was the minor lairds, both blue bonneted and red, who did the most for their properties and for those who lived on them, the red-hatted particularly since they were the King's

Cromarty House

servants and, until 1746, the administrators of justice. A slightly later example exists at Cromarty, north of Inverness, on the Black Isle. This had been the barony of the Urquharts of that Ilk, including Sir Thomas Urquhart, the cavalier who translated *Rabelais* into his native tongue and is reputed to have died of laughter on hearing of the Restoration of Charles II. He lived in Cromarty Castle, but that was demolished in the eighteenth century by the Rosses, who succeeded as feudal barons in the district, and it was this family which made the burgh a model one and built Cromarty House in the purest Adam style. It must be the most northerly of such exercises. Cromarty was almost completely rebuilt, with pleasant Georgian houses, a splendid little court house where the baronial justice would be meted out, a manse and kirk, wherein the laird and his family could sit in their loft, or private box, and see that everyone behaved. There was also a Gaelic chapel for the Highlanders for whom work was found in a brewery which was to take the place of whisky distilling and hopefully discourage spiritous consumption amongst the incomers!

Cromarty House was built in the mid-1770s, the mason and designer probably being Robert Wright, who worked for Robert Adam in the New Town of Edinburgh and also at Culloden House, nearer Inverness. His presence there no doubt made it easier for him to come still further north. It stands on a bluff above

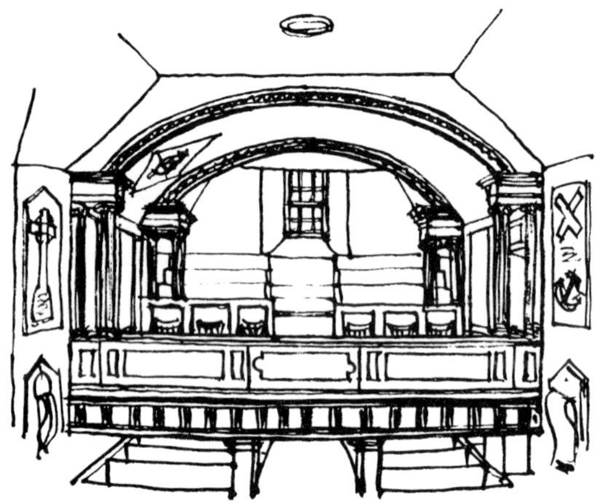

Laird's loft, Cromarty kirk

the little burgh and is reached both by road and, the back door, by a short-cut tunnel, which radical sentimentalists insist was so that the servants could not be seen by the family and their guests as they came and went but which almost certainly was for safety reasons and possibly also occasionally to assist smuggling. The last Ross superior has now gone, but not before erecting in the middle of the kitchen garden, down in the town, a brash modern house with a green roof, instead of accepting a grant to restore a charming seventeenth-century house nearby which badly needed saving and which would have made a delightful home, with character, for anyone. The barony has since been acquired by Mr Michael Nightingale, from the south of England, who is now properly known as Nightingale of Cromarty and is keen to keep up the house and play what role he can in the burgh of which he is feudal baron.

The Adam family originally worked in the north of Scotland as

Garden front, Newliston, West Lothian

employees of the Board of Ordnance, principally at Fort George, between Nairn and Inverness, and this had several significant results: it led to important commissions from the lords of the establishment, if one can use such a phrase, and it instilled in Robert Adam an understanding of military architecture, which, when added to his subsequently acquired appreciation of Italian castles and Roman remains, such as the sea-front Palace of Diocletian, at Spalato (Split), in Dalmatia, produced towards the end of his life that marvellous castellated style which so surpassed anything the Gothic revivalists themselves were doing as to be something entirely on its own and virtually unique to Adam himself. In his youth he had considered Scotland 'but a narrow place', but the success of the Strawberry Hill medievalists and other latter-day eclectics in south Britain, plus financial difficulties consequent upon the failure of the Adelphi project, sent him scuttling home, back to that 'narrow place' where for the last decade of his life he worked harder and possibly more rewardingly than ever before.

I will return to Robert Adam's castellated style, really military

in the broadest sense and not just a thing of pointed windows and crenellations, which in fact he used sparingly, in the next chapter, when I come to deal with the return to romanticism and the eclipse of both Palladian and neo-classical architecture. Meantime there is Newliston to describe. This was Adam's last house, a comparatively modest one, otherwise it would have no place here amongst Scottish baronial manors, and it was built while Charlotte Square in Edinburgh was being laid out very much in the same style—indeed, the southern façade might almost have been taken from an end pavilion of that square. Robert Adam died in 1792, when Charlotte Square and Newliston alike were not quite finished. The square was not satisfactorily completed, only the north side being as intended, and the inferior Robert Reid redesigned Adam's fine St George's Church in lumpy, top-heavy style. Newliston was luckier, the unfinished bits were inside, and even so that interior is perhaps one of the architect's most restrained and chaste creations anywhere. Bryce came along in the mid-nineteenth century and altered a few things, adding wings and a terrace and providing stances for two stone hogs, the crest of the then owners. He also designed a baronial lodge which has all the faults and misunderstandings of the ready-made and which, although described as Franco-Scottish in style, is in neither.

Newliston was originally a Dundas property and is not far from their ancient seat, Dundas Castle, but it came to the Dalrymples of Stair in 1669 when the heiress married Sir John Dalrymple, later first Earl of Stair and father of Field Marshal Lord Stair, British Ambassador to France. Sir John Dalrymple was the man chiefly responsible for the Massacre of Glencoe. He was an avid supporter of the Revolution of 1688 and callously made use of the animosity between clans Campbell and MacDonald to have the latter, the poorer and weaker, made an example of by the former, and thus secure the Highlands for William of Orange.

The house which Stair came to at Newliston was an old laird's tower which his son, the second Earl, commissioned William Adam to replace and to plant around with extensive avenues and water-gardens. These, based to some extent on what Stair had seen whilst ambassador at Versailles, in part survive, in part only

Bryce's 'baronial' lodge, Newliston

because the trees and shrubs have got a bit overgrown and it is now difficult to see exactly what the pattern on the ground is really meant to be. There was a legend, for instance, that the various rather enigmatic clearances to the east of the house represented the layout of the troops at the Battle of Dettingen, in which the Field Marshal participated, but clearly this is impossible, for no battle array was ever as symmetrical as this; the late Roger Hog told me that the whole story had 'come up the back stairs via a Sunday school teacher'. The layout in question is actually of the Union Jack, and the *grand pièce d'eau* in front of the house is almost certainly inspired by Versailles or Vaux-le-Vicomte.

William Adam's house was never built and, the Field Marshal dying without a son, the property was sold to the Hogs, whose descendants still live there. They were merchants from London and employed the greatest architect of the age, Robert Adam, to design this house for them. How lucky they were. The grounds were already planned and planted, William Adam's stables existed plus a double doocot from the old laird's tower, and Robert Adam was at the height of his powers, working with his usual craftsmen only a few miles away in Edinburgh. Both house and formal layout of grounds are aligned to specific points, the grounds with Craighall, to the east, the house with Hopetoun, the bow window on the garden side facing towards that larger mansion. The result of this is that layout and houses are askew, or perhaps one should say that the vista programmes were at variance, each being done at a different period for different reasons. Inside Newliston all is purity of line and aristocratic refinement, Roman in the best sense, with Pompeian details to lighten the severe effect of Doric columns and chimneypieces. There were even two needlework panels designed to be worked by the lady of the house, pelmets, and hangings for a four-poster bed, not to mention three chaste gilt mirrors and a set of painted chairs.

In place of so much restraint and patrician good taste, David Bryce was allowed to enlarge the ballroom in 1845; it is not much more in keeping with the rest of the interior than his baronial east lodge is with the remaining lodges of William Adam. I suppose one could say that, since there was an earlier Scottish baronial

Lorimer's North Lodge, Balcarres House, Fife: compare it with Newliston

house at Newliston, a baronial lodge is not entirely inappropriate, but the thing is, does it express the spirit of that earlier style or merely the letter? The answer to this question can best be found by making an invidious comparison, by looking at another baronialist, only of this century not the last. I refer to a work of Sir Robert Lorimer.

Lorimer was clearly a romanticist and just as likely to misunderstand a piece of classical architecture as Bryce, but he did appreciate the true native ethos, and traditional craftsmanship. Hence, if we look at his north lodge at Balcarres, we can see at once what is meant by Baronial, and Scots Baronial at that. This delightful adjunct to an otherwise uninteresting and over-large country house, with its south lodge in red brick and looking as if it came from the Home Counties, conjures up the whole spirit of sixteenth-century Scotland in its combined suggestions of Queen Mary's bath-house at Holyrood and a miniscule laird's tower, and even more especially in the architect's clever use of the baronial heraldry. The Lindsay supporting lion holds aloft in gilded iron the swan crest of that family, whilst the curving wall leading to the gate is pierced in alternate voids and solids to represent the fesse-chequey of their coat of arms.

6. Transformations

Long before Voltaire had Rousseau's Social Contract publicly burnt, or the so-called 'Return to Nature' movement had made bohemianism respectable, there had been growing resistance to the rigidities of Palladianism and to the strict neo-classical code. Even Vanbrugh himself had shown the way, not only by contorting Palladio's ideas but by introducing Gothic suggestions of manner and shape. He designed the first military barracks, as such, in Britain, at Berwick-upon-Tweed, and in 1726 produced a scheme for a new castle for the Duke of Argyll at Inveraray. Earlier, in 1718, he had worked with William Adam at Floors in Berwickshire, vast castellated seat of the dukes of Roxburghe. Vanbrugh's Inveraray plan was not followed up, at least not at the time, but it was copied (or should we say 'studied'?) by Roger Morris, 'Carpenter and Engineer' to the Board of Ordnance and, therefore, a fellow worker at Fort George and elsewhere with William Adam and his sons, John and Robert; it was with William and John Adam that Morris was employed by a later Duke of Argyll to start building a new Campbell castle at Inveraray. The old castle further up the shores of Loch Fyne was abandoned, the village was pulled down and rebuilt on a grid plan by Robert Mylne on a new site, and new Inveraray Castle begun in 1744, work continuing throughout the Forty-five rebellion.

The castle was foursquare, with false 'keep' in the centre, and four round, crenellated corner towers, had pointed windows and was surrounded by a dry moat or *fosse*. It was entirely English in character but in due course a few Scotticisms were added, such as whimpled roofs and typical dormer windows, though in general it remains as designed, complete with superb Adamesque interiors, actually the work of Robert Mylne. All this predated Strawberry Hill and most other southern essays in similar vein by many years, and any native Scottish attempts at medievalism by even more. The fact that Inveraray was built during the Forty-five had something to do with this, since the Campbells were the largest and most powerful clan in Scotland on the Hanoverian side and could, possibly alone, have proceeded on such a venture at such at time. Yet it is remarkable how quickly the wounds of Culloden and 'Butcher Cumberland's' reprisals healed, and by

Inveraray Castle

the end of the century even Achnacarry, burnt-out seat of the Camerons of Lochiel, principal opponents of the Campbells and chief sufferers amongst Prince Charles Edward's erstwhile adherents, was rebuilt.

The architect of Achnacarry was a youthful James Gillespie, not yet with the affix Graham, and its frame, though classical, is ornamented with Gothic detail, turrets and crenellations. It is the sort of house that had appeared a few years before in the south, based on Robert Adam's large castles at Culzean, Seton and Wedderburn, a good example of which is the Gothic villa erected by Charles Gordon of Cluny, who acquired the barony of Braid in 1770 and employed Robert Burn, father of William Burn, the foremost of the Battle-of-the-Styles architects of the following century, to design it. Until a few years Hermitage of Braid was still private property, but it is now in a public park belonging to Edinburgh Corporation and rather wasted; it has its doocot, sure

Hermitage of Braid, Edinburgh, a baronial villa

sign of an older property, and its amusing story of Joanna, known as 'Jacky', daughter of Charles Gordon, who married the future seventh Earl of Stair in 1804. He succeeded in 1807 whilst abroad, where he made a bigamous alliance with a Miss Manners, only to have that annulled when he returned. Unhappily his former marriage was also subsequently annulled, so he was married to no one and 'Jacky' had to spend the rest of her life immured at Hermitage of Braid.

One of the curious things about the Adam family was that, although they inspired and built for others, at Blair Adam, which was their Kinrossshire estate, they never managed to erect anything much for themselves. William Adam bought the property and built a few cottages at the entrance to what was then, and still is, only an enlarged farmhouse, calling the settlement Maryburgh, and it was 'of Maryburgh' that he styled himself. Further, to emphasize links with the past (one of the Adams had actually fallen at Flodden), he purchased Dowhill Castle from the Lyndsays. This was a genuine medieval ruin and stood on the edge of the Blair Adam Estate. He gave it to Robert, who made it just a little more genuine so as to fulfil current ideas of a Gothic folly, but they still built no baronial manor house. A number of schemes were prepared at different times by different members of the family, including one by Robert Adam to convert Blair into a smaller version of Sir John Clerk's Mavisbank, and there were

Dowhill Castle, 'medieval ruin', Blair Adam

to be thatched and Swiss cottages, rustic gates and lodge and a new Maryburgh, laid out in a formal pattern. None of this materialized, though the estate does have an English park and is famous for its woods. The house also preserves interesting drawings and portraits, and there are some contemporary ornamental features in the grounds.

William Adam, as previously mentioned, was much influenced by Vanbrugh and reputedly worked with him at Floors Castle, in Berwickshire; yet, apart from his military work and assistance as Master of Works at Inveraray, he does not seem to have been much interested in the new-fangled Gothic taste that had begun to infiltrate north shortly before his death in 1748. Indeed, Robert Adam himself, though he eventually outstripped the rest of them, did not at first take to this fake medievalism. William Adam went on building in the antique style almost without knowing it, while clothing his buildings with an elaborate veneer of classicism. Thus Duff House, which with its square plan and domed corner towers is not really so very different from Inveraray Castle, except that it had Baroque details and the other 'Gothycke'.

Nearby, in the town of Banff, is a much less demonstrative William Adam house called Banff Castle. It stands on part of the

Town house by William Adam on the site of Banff Castle

site of a fortress erected by Edward I of England, of which a tiny postern gate survives, and is as plain and wholesome as any James Smith or early Bruce house, with hipped roof and nicely placed chimneys, and harled, with margins around windows and at the corners, but otherwise without any extraneous decoration. It was the town house of the Findlaters, one of the local families who spent the winter in Banff and made of it a little centre of culture on the model of some Continental towns, and is one of the subjects bought by a thriving Preservation Society which buys up threatened properties, restores them and then re-sells.

William Adam was also engaged by Lady Grisel Baillie to design a house on the Mavisbank model for her at Mellerstain, in Berwickshire, and the two side wings for this were built before the estate went to a nephew who changed his architect and style of architecture. He had been on the Grand Tour, and no one less than the great Robert Adam himself would do. The result is one of that architect's earliest and most ambitious works in the

castellated manner, though more of the authentic Robert Adam designs seem to be inside, where the library is considered his finest room north of the Border. The exterior may have been partly the work of the owner himself, for the plans are signed by him, and really the elevations are not up to Robert Adam's best. Too big for further discussion here, one might just add that one brilliant idea Adam did carry out at Mellerstain was the creation of a long gallery running through the western bay of the building with windows at both ends and along the whole of one side; it is gently barrel-vaulted with elegant peristyles and Pompeian decoration.

In the same county, just outside Duns, is Wedderburn Castle, another Robert Adam building but wholly his, very large and built by James Nisbet, a mason from Kelso. Whether it is mere coincidence or not, neighbouring Nisbet House ends in an Adam crenellated tower that might have come direct from Wedderburn, and boasts internal plasterwork probably of the same provenance. The tower stands at the western end of the building as one approaches it, almost hiding a typical laird's 'keep' of the sixteenth century, while just peeping round the corner, so to speak, is one of two round, conically capped towers which Sir Alexander Nisbet erected in the seventeenth century when he replaced an older redoubt belonging to the Kers, whose motto survives above the original entrance. The last time I saw Nisbet it looked rather forlorn, some nineteenth-century additions had been demolished and the rest clearly needed renovating and occupying. It is now to be restored with the aid of a Ministry grant and should be one of the pleasantest houses of its kind to live in when finished.

Wedderburn seems more in line with Robert Adam's interest in the work of the Board of Ordnance, or even the *castelli romani*, than anything produced by the more mundane, though often more celebrated, architects of the Gothycke Revival. The end tower at Nisbet seems almost to reverse the more common arrangement of leaving an ancient 'keep' at one end and adding to it, for, of course, it is the newest part. There are many old houses which began with a fortified tower to which was added a manor in the sixteenth or later centuries, the most obvious being Drum, in

Nisbet House, Berwickshire: a castellated addition to the laird's tower

The old keep at Gleneagles, with banner of 26th laird

Aberdeenshire, already mentioned, and somewhere the old tower has been left as a kind of folly at some distance from the new house.

Gleneagles, in Perthshire, is such a case. The barony has been in the hands of the Haldane family for at least seven hundred years, almost as long as any other in the country, certainly if one counts being on the same land and not merely in Scotland. They were not an especially remarkable family in the early days, though latterly they produced a bishop of Argyll and the Isles of quite extraordinary character, a man who combined the life of a Highland chief, his piper playing him into dinner, with that of a fatherly prelate, 'the second St Columba' as he was called, who revived religious life on Iona. The religious side of the Haldanes came out also in two Haldane brothers who became missionaries in India and rabid tractarians for extreme Protestantism! The same two men commissioned Robert Adam to design Airthrey Castle for them in his best Culzean style, then paid him for the sketch and employed his masons to do the work for them. More amusingly they advertised for a resident hermit to come and live in their new hermitage, and got a reply! Airthrey was smaller than Culzean and unfortunately fell victim to baronialization in the nineteenth century, which completely spoilt its whole conception. It is now within Stirling University.

Another family whose residence on the same land goes back a very long way are the Brodies, who claim never to have had any

Corner of Brodie House, Nairn, before harling

predecessors. It is only unfortunate that the present Brodie of Brodie could not persuade any of his relations to come and succeed him and therefore had little choice but to hand the property over to the National Trust with himself as tenant. It is even more unfortunate what they have done to the appearance of the House of Brodie. This began life as the usual tower of defence, with sixteenth-century additions, but during Montrose's campaigns the place was largely destroyed and had to be rebuilt. The nucleus of the old tower survived and some of it is still standing, with the restored portion and additions at one side. Here two sets of plasterers worked, sophisticated Renaissance ones who did

Lochnaw, Wigtonshire: old tower and Caroline mansion

the dining-room, and the more old-fashioned variety who did some pre-Civil War work on one of the barrel-vaulted ceilings. The first must surely be the farthest north reached by the Holyrood apprentices, for that is who they must have been, coming perhaps via Fyvie from Arbuthnott and possibly Brechin Castle, which was rebuilt by a pupil of Sir William Bruce's in the late seventeenth century.

The real disaster at Brodie has been the harling, for now the building is a fraud, in the sense that, instead of showing its age and history in its masonry, the entire building, including a large nineteenth-century addition by William Burn, has been harled. This disaster has now been recognized in official circles, but there is nothing that can be done. Even to remove the harling from one wall of Pittenweem Priory would cost nearly £30,000, so what it would be for a whole mansion house I shudder to think.

Speaking of harling brings me to Lochnaw, right down in the south-west, near Stranraer. The old tower there has just escaped a harling, which at first was made the *quid pro quo* for an Historic

Kilravock, Nairn, sixteenth, seventeenth and eighteenth centuries

Buildings grant. Happily the private Trust that owns Lochnaw did not give in without a fight and, after getting first-rate and authoritative advice, was able to have the tower 'point harled' instead—that is, to have the joints pointed in a harl mixture to match the stonework and so leave it looking more or less as it was before, but actually stronger and more weathertight. They also found some Jacobean painted beams in the tower, which have been restored. The date of the tower in question is open to doubt, but since the Agnews, whose seat this was until Sir Fulques Agnew sold the barony to Sir Charles Hambro before the last war, were made sherrifs of Wigton in the mid-fifteenth century, I think one can assume it dates from some time after that, or just before. The rest of the building, the inhabited part, was built in the second half of the seventeenth century, and another wing in the first half of the eighteenth, there was a chapel attached to that which was demolished more recently. In fact, the whole castle and adjuncts were in danger of demolition when the present proprietors bought it from Sir Charles Hambro and so saved it for posterity. They were lucky, incidentally, that previously Sir Charles had demolished an enormous early nineteenth-century addition in Irish Gothic, with stepped-up crenellations and huge towers and mini-keeps that completely dominated everything for miles around.

The Roses of Kilravock do still live on their ancestral lands, near Nairn, in their ancient tower of defence, permission to build which was granted, not by the King but by the Lord of Isles, in 1460. This is about the time most stone towers were erected in Scotland, and it would seem reasonable, therefore, that the one at Lochnaw also dates from around the same date, though the owners place it earlier, and the Ministry later. In any event, there is no doubt about the authenticity of the charter of 1460 which grants Hugh Rose (every Rose is called Hugh and has been until quite recently), the right to 'upmak a toure of fens with barmkin'. The Roses came to Scotland in the wake of the Norman invasion of England and were undoubtedly settled near Nairn by 1230; the barony was created in 1295. One does not quite know what they lived in before 1460 but presumably in a pele, or tower of timber, as their Border brethren did, for most of the Normans in northern Scotland came from the Borders, not directly from the south of England or Normandy. To this tower another Hugh Rose added his manor house, which he linked to the 'keep' rather cleverly with a square tower containing scale-and-platt stairs.

In Georgian times other improvements and small additions were made to create the attractive house we see today, a castle completely transformed to domestic purposes, picturesque but comfortable, harled in its newer parts and left to speak for its antiquity in others. It is reached down a long, straight avenue, a cul de sac—hence, perhaps, its lesser fame than that of neighbouring Cawdor Castle, some of whose masons were engaged at both buildings in the fifteenth century. Miss Rose runs it as a 'Christian Guest House', but what its fate may be eventually one does not really know. Mary, Queen of Scots, and Bonnie Prince Charlie both stayed here at different times, and also 'Butcher Cumberland', the night after Culloden. He must, at least, have had some sense of humour, heavy and German if you like, but on greeting the then Hugh Rose he remarked: 'I hear you have been entertaining my cousin.' Better than having him locked up and his lands sequestered.

Old Manor of Allardyce: detail of corbelling

Still more ancient families of Norman descent, or Saxon, living on long-acquired ancestral lands and in evolved or much transformed manor houses, are to be found in Kincardineshire and Angus. The Arbuthnotts, whose real name was Olifard, and that probably derived from Oliphant, were already in Glen Bervie when Hugo de Swinton came from the Borders to marry the heiress in the eleventh century. The de Swintons themselves survived, *in situ*, at Swinton, in Berwickshire, until quite recently, when the last baron, the late Canon Alan Swinton, died. The local kirk is full of souvenirs, including a number of carved boars, the family crest, and the recumbent figure of 'Alanus Svintonus Miles de Eodem', the last part of the Latin tag supposedly representing the old Scots form 'of that Ilk'. Indeed, the Swintons of that Ilk are said to possess the most ancient charter in the country, going back to the days when Anglo-Saxon kings ruled south-east Scotland (Bernicia) from the Tyne to the Forth, with Edinburgh as their capital. Arbuthnott is almost certainly a Pictish name and originally spelt with an 'h' at the end,

Arbuthnott House, Kincardineshire: seventeenth-century wing

like Arbroath; it is sometimes also spelt with only one 't', as it is in the case of one of my ancestresses. It was, of course, simply the territorial form adopted by the Olifards, and then the de Swintons, after a stay of a few hundred years in Glen Bervie, where they subsequently vied with the Allardyces, just down the burn towards the sea, in fulfilling the role of local lairds, co-founding the beautiful little fortified kirk at Arbuthnott, with its 'Beauvais' apse, medieval tombs and unique 'priest's flat'.

The harled and whitewashed seat of the Allardyces has been restored, not by them (they became extinct in the main line some time ago) but by people from Aberdeen, who have done it nicely, leaving at least some stonework to speak for itself. Most of the house is domestic and not particularly old but there survives a perfectly splendid example of late sixteenth-century Scottish corbelling on the inside of the oldest bit, the pended entrance, with two amusing turrets poking up above. This particular corbelling has been likened to 'Arab work' and is certainly both extremely decorative and clever. Nothing like it remains at

Georgian façade, Arbuthnott House

Arbuthnott, although almost all the original tour of defence is still there, hidden behind several skins of seventeenth-, eighteenth- and even nineteenth-century work, for here we have the evolved building *par excellence*. The entrance porch belongs to the last century, the main façade to the century before and the garden side to the sixteenth and seventeenth centuries, with thick walls and shot-holes redolent of earlier times. Gradually the 'castle' of the de Swintons lost its towers and its turrets, and eventually its courtyard, which was filled in and the house no longer approached, as Allardyce still is, via a pend and gatehouse. The garden, incidentally, was laid out in Restoration times, though not so extensively as Pitmedden.

The plainish seventeenth-century wing contains the most sumptuous 'Holrood' ceilings, but as the rooms are low they seem rather overbearing and heavy, instead of light and fanciful, while some of their features are odd in the extreme. Lady Arbuthnott says that the grapes had become raspberries by the time they reached the Mearns, as this district is called, but there

Brechin Castle, *c.*1700

are even more peculiar things than that, half-eagle, half-cherub-like creatures that suggest moulds from Prestonfield or some other contemporary house having got very badly mixed by the 'sorcerer's apprentices'. In the later addition, which was built by a mason from Montrose, whose bills survive, are more sophisticated decorations and *objets d'art*. Five Jacobite portraits tell of the family's allegiances, though they did manage to circumvent trouble by half of them supporting Bonnie Prince Charlie while the others did not. The hall is one of three important specimens in a particular genre—that is, of a lowish, largish entrance with ceremonial stairs, reached through a peristyle, or columned opening, at the back. The others are at Brechin Castle, not far away, and at Touch House, near Stirling. The first was designed by Alexander Edwards, a pupil of Bruce, the second by a young John Adam, working after his father's demise in 1748.

The sixteenth laird of Arbuthnott was created first Viscount by Charles I; the fourteenth Viscount did obeisance on behalf of his fellow viscounts (Lord Falkland being absent) at the coronation of Her Majesty the Queen in 1953.

Brechin Castle is built on the site of a very much earlier fortalice, possibly even of a Pictish fort, for this was a great Pictish centre and a cathedral 'city' boasting a pre-Norman round tower, which is still hale. The rebuilt cathedral and tower stand on one side of the ravine made by the River Esk, the castle on the other, making a fine architectural and historic site, though neither, except for a few details, is as old or romantic as it looks. The castle was the seat of the Maules, who became earls of Panmure and strong Jacobites, and was built in its present form by the fourth Earl. He fell out with James VII and II, as nearly everyone did if they did not share his faith, and retiring to the country set about rebuilding his seat, de-castellating it almost completely except for the *tour de rigueur* peeping out from behind the new work. Brechin Castle is approached via a splendid avenue and looks almost exactly like a French *château*, with its classical centre-piece, pediment and conically capped end towers. It is, in fact, much more like a French *château* than any of the more elaborate Scottish baronial exercises in Aberdeenshire, which are often said to be French inspired, though they are not.

The architect of Brechin Castle was Alexander Edward, son of a parson and one himself, a non-juror and episcopalian but more interested in the arts. In 1696 he is mentioned as going to Hopetoun with 'the Lord Rankeillor (a Law Lord and brother of Sir Thomas Hope of Craighall), and Sir William Bruce . . . Great Masters of Architecture and Contrivances of Avenue, Gardens and Orchards'. He is also known for having made a drawing of Bruce's design for Kinross, including the gardens and out-buildings. This must be amongst the very first such architectural plans made in Scotland.

Tobias Bauchop, Bruce's own mason from Alloa, in Clackman-nanshire, did some of the work at Brechin; also a William Walker from Pillivie, who is reputed to have made the wrought ironwork for the ceremonial stairs. I say 'reputed' because the design seems later than that which would have been in fashion in Scotland in the reign of Queen Anne. In fact, it looks Georgian and may, therefore, replace the original. Certainly upstairs there has been a considerable change, for that is all Victorian Tudor! That happened long after the Maules had disappeared from the scene. The Earl proclaimed James VIII and III at the Mercat Cross in Brechin in 1715 and actually entertained the 'Old Pretender' in his new house a year later, after having fought and been wounded at the Battle of Sherrifmuir, for all of which he and his family were forced to leave the country. He died in France in 1723.

Touch House near Stirling was a Seton seat, a cadet branch of that celebrated family, untitled and not so much involved in history as their cousins, yet interesting and gifted in their own way and resident here on the same site from the fourteenth century till about fifty years ago. The barony was symbolized, as were so many others, with a tower of defence which is still standing, at one side of a more modern mansion and linked behind with sixteenth- and seventeenth-century buildings. An early Seton was a particular companion of James IV and died at Flodden, while another was heavily fined by Cromwell, though more for his absences than attendances for he really did nothing very much to aid the cause of Charles I. Later, his successor was also punished for not attending some official function in the days of William of Orange, and in the eighteenth century, after some support for the Jacobite cause, Hugh Seton settled down to husbandry and the building of the present handsome Adam main house.

For some time Touch House was thought to have been designed by William Adam, but apart from the fact that its date is later than 1748, it is not heavy enough for him, except possibly in certain details, such as the lumpy but inadequate front door and the way in which the upper windows seem to hang from the similarly inadequate entablature. A recent discovery by the present owner shows that the architect was John Adam, still finding his way as an architect and not yet having handed over to brother Robert and retired to deal with the Blair Adam estate as he was to do. Inside, too, the name of Thomas Clayton, William Adam's plasterer, has been established, the work, however, being much more refined than heretofore, or even as at Blair Castle, in Perthshire, where Clayton also worked without William Adam in charge.

Hugh Seton eventually came to grief: he over-borrowed and left the country, ending up in oriental disguise in the Near East, but his house is all there. The family retrieved the situation, and when their descendants died out, it went to newcomers who have looked after it extremely well, and especially since Sir Robert Lorimer had a go at it and was prevented by fate, his

Touch, Stirling, an Adam house attached to an old tower

demise in 1929, from doing too much. A lodge in the usual Lorimer manner was built and looks all right, though I am told it is not so good inside. This was a common fault with architects earlier this century: Sir Edwin Lutyens was always getting into trouble with the position of WCs and other necessities for which he had not planned. At Touch House Lorimer's chief function was to scrape off the dark stain from the handsome panelling inside and generally tidy up the interior where it needed it, while making the exterior uniform by putting astragals in all the windows, in place of Victorian plate glass, and so adding to the pretence, so much in evidence elsewhere these days, that the whole building was built at the same time. Happily Lorimer was no harler, otherwise we might have seen another Brodie! One interesting point that may escape the casual observer concerns the architect's use of four glazing bars in his windows instead of the more usual three. Georgian windows were hardly ever square and always divided into threes, while late Stewart ones

Bannockburn House

were more often square, or nearly so, and were divided into four, as here, and the glazing bars were heavier.

Touch is very similar—its Georgian façade, that is—to Durie House, in Fife, and one wonders if some new discovery there will establish the same Adam brother at work. The finely sculpted tympanum, incidentally, displays the arms of Hugh Seton and his wife, Elizabeth. The Setons had been Armour Bearers to the King, and this office was recognized in a charter of Charles II dated 1672, the salary being paid until the end of Stuart rule, since when both office and salary have been either in dispute or dormant, partly as the result of the family's Jacobite leanings. The marriage of Hugh and Elizabeth Seton took place on the very day of Prestonpans, a reference to which appears in the kirk register in which the minister, obviously also Jacobite inclined, wrote 'Glory to God in the Highest'. Bonnie Prince Charlie actually stayed at Touch in the same year, and his bedroom is maintained as such. There is also an amusing story told of how, some twenty years after the Forty-five, there was held a ball in the drawing-room at Touch in which two ancient aunts of Hugh Seton and one nonagenarian uncle danced reels energetically together, one of the aunts being the mother of Charles Edward's mistress Clementina Walkinshaw.

The association between Hugh Seton's aunt and Prince Charlie is, perhaps, worth a brief retelling, especially since it brings in another manor house in the same district, Bannockburn House. The existing rather depressing building, almost wholly surrounded by the contortions of a motorway and its junctions on the outskirts of Stirling and overlooked by every passing vehicle, dates from the seventeenth century, with later 'improvements', *circa* 1768. The barony was given by Charles I to Lord Rollo, whose son sold it to Hugh Paterson, and that is where the Seton connection begins for the first Hugh Seton (there were two in succession), was a Paterson of Bannockburn, and indeed the nonagenarian uncle indulging in balletic high jinks at Touch in 1766 was none other than Sir Hugh Paterson of Bannockburn. They built the house, Sir Hugh's initials being on it, and endowed it with a magnificent fretwork ceiling in the drawing-room reminiscent of that in the music room at Holyrood. There is also a doocot nearby dated 1698. Prince Charlie stayed in the house on two occasions, on his way south in 1745 and on his return to Scotland a year later, and is said then to have seduced Clementina Walkinshaw. Clementina was a niece of Sir Hugh and is supposed to have been staying in the house with her mother, a Walkinshaw of Barrowfield, a neighbouring property, and that is why the ninety-seven-year-old lady dancing the reel at Touch was known as 'Lady' Barrowfield.

One should further explain that the first Hugh, born a Paterson of Bannockburn, like the second, Hugh Smith, took Elizabeth Seton's name on marrying her, she being the heiress of Touch. The Paterson house is now in a sorry state; it has had a fire, if not two, and is only half-occupied; its site is against its being bought and restored as well, though, since it has a preservation order on it, it may survive a few more years.

Perhaps the most dramatic metamorphosis of all Scottish castles and houses was that of the sixteenth-century tower of the Stewarts of Atholl at Blair, which the Murrays, when they got it first, turned into an enlarged laird's manor house, then almost pulled down completely, lopping off the battlements and upper stories before rebuilding the place as an English country house.

This was in the time of the Hanoverian Duke of Atholl who outbid his relations over Nairne House and demolished it. He was a Stanley by marriage, a family that held the former Kingship of Man and has left at least one happy reminder of that in 'The Whim', a one-walled folly on a hillside above Blair designed like a

'The Whim', Blair Castle

toy fort and flying from the highest point the three-legged flag of the Isle of Man. Blair had been besieged by his Jacobite brother, the last real siege on the British mainland, and perhaps that inspired him in his dislike of the Stuarts and all they stood for, and also caused him to eradicate any Murray connection after the failure of their cause. In any event, he did so, only to be spited in return by a later duke, who had the English country house transformed back into a Scottish castle, the architect being the ubiquitous baronializer David Bryce, who here did quite a good job. He put back the battlements of the old Comyn Tower and rebuilt the rest of Blair in suitable style, complete with arched entrance feature copied from Fyvie.

Smaller gentry, such as the Drummonds of Hawthornden, did not rise to such prodigious works, like others previously mentioned; they were not rich enough to enlarge their property, nor so poor they needed to sell any of it, but managed to maintain it reasonable well. The castle of Hawthornden, near Edinburgh, is old and represented today as a separate, semi-ruined tower at one side of a largely seventeenth-century replacement. It retains its pit prison, or dungeon, where the feudal baron, in exercising his appointed duties, held miscreants awaiting sentence; beside it is the ancient sycamore tree beneath which Sir William

Hawthornden, Midlothian, showing part of the *enceinte* and later house

Drummond, the Cavalier poet and rebuilder of Hawthornden, sat and discoursed with Ben Jonson. One enters the newer manor house through the original gateway, with arm-length bolt still closing the inner courtyard each night, and once inside the remains of a medieval *enceinte* (enclosing wall), line the edge of the red cliffs below on one side of the two-sided seventeenth-century building.

The site is extremely old, said to be Pictish, with caves made long ago by Bruce's paladin, the house itself also treasuring Bruce's sword, until the death of Sir James Williams-Drummond, who had no heir and intended to leave Hawthornden to the National Trust for Scotland. In the event they never got it, since, as he told me himself, the representative who came to look at it seemed much more interested in living in the house himself than anything else. Since then a number of people have gone there, and its future is by no means secure, not only for the more obvious reasons but for more literal ones, of vandalism and theft. Sir James always slept with his shotgun at his side!

The 'Bonnie Hoose O'Airlie', pronounced 'Eroly' and originally spelt that way, is one of the best-loved and romanticized places in Scotland, noted for the Ogilvy loyalty to the Crown, their exile abroad in the wake of that loyalty, their revival and the more recent marriage between the brother of the present Earl of Airlie, the Hon. Angus Ogilvy, to HRH Princess Alexandra. There is much poetry in the legends and stories about this

Airlie Castle, Angus

staunch family and its much-destroyed and much-rebuilt seat. One recalls the terrible Battle of Arbroath in 1445, in which the Lindsays and the Ogilvies decimated each other, the chief of the Lindsays himself dying in the fray, wherein five hundred Ogilvies were slain. The well-known couplet:

> An Ogilvy in green
> Should never be seen

is supposed to refer to the green in their tartan, which was blamed for so many deaths, but was probably something else, as clan tartans of any colour scarcely existed in the fifteenth century. In any event, they now appear in checks of blue, yellow and red, just in case. In the seventeenth century Argyll came to hack down Airlie Castle, wielding an axe with the rest of the demolishers, taking advantage of the absence abroad of James, Earl of Airlie, to browbeat his young son and mother and get rid of an adversary's seat at the same time.

Airlie Castle, a small Regency House attached to the restored gatehouse

> The lady look'd o'er the hie Castle wa'
> And, Oh! but she signed sairly,
> When she saw Argyle and a' his men
> To plunder the Bonnie Hoose
> O'Airlie.

The civil war was like this, of course, but it is interesting to note that, although Argyll took his vengeance on the Airlies and Airlie Castle was almost entirely ruined, when Oliver Cromwell's man, General Monk, came to Cortachy, whence Lady Airlie and her son had fled, he only 'slighted' it (dismantled its defences) as ordered, and any pilfering or damage that occurred was dealt with afterwards in proper army fashion. Monk was not involved in Scottish family feuds.

All that remained of Airlie Castle after Argyll's visitation was the entrance gateway and one adjacent length of wall, and so it remained until the end of the eighteenth century, when 'Le Bell Ecossais', as the fifth Earl was called in France, where he lived for many years in exile, returned home and began repairing his damaged and nearly ruined patrimony. The manor house he built at Airlie is very much in the local style, quite plain, two-storeyed with vaulted basement, and attics, and is not so very different from a large Angus farmhouse of the late Georgian period. It runs at right angles to the old gatehouse and defence wall and provides the second side of a garden courtyard, the other sides falling away steeply to two streams that meet below. It is a perfect defensive site even today, for once the gate is closed there is no way into that peaceful haven. That is perhaps why Airlie has provided so excellent a retreat for three successive dowager ladies, the Liberal Blanche who nearly ruined the family with her Gladstonian house-parties at Cortachy and who had ambitious plans to rebuild Airlie as a nineteenth-century baronial edifice; Mabell, who resembled the late Queen Mary and was one of the royal ladies in waiting, working with the Queen tapestries for the chairs at Holyrood and undertaking other artistic ploys; and the late Bridget, whose death in 1984 has left the dower house temporarily without a tenant.

The simplicity of the fifth Earl's rebuilding was such that there was not even a front hall to Airlie, the present one having been made out of the dining-room, when eating and cooking moved downstairs to the vaulted basement. On the stair was an enigmatic portrait of a young sixteenth-century girl who Lady Airlie used to think might be Marion Ogilvy who married Cardinal Beaton before he took Holy Orders, or was his mistress afterwards, no one seems quite sure, but for whom Melgund was certainly built. The story is less well authenticated than the one about 'Le Bell Ecossais' who, before he took a mistress in France, wrote to his wife in Scotland and asked her permission to do so. She willingly agreed and when he returned from exile they were duly reunited just as if nothing had happened. Another thing he did then was to begin laying out the garden which today is so much appreciated and which is said to incorporate the Battle of Waterloo in its plan. This seems no more likely than that Dettingen was planned at Newliston, for again the scheme is completely symmetrical, and therefore 'French', but nothing to do with battles. There is also one of the very few genuine parterres here, made with tiny hedges and coloured patterns of gravel and appropriate plants which are such a feature of the

Continent and are wasted unless one can see them from above. Here that problem is solved by laying the formal pattern out on a slope.

If Countess Blanche's Whig parties nearly ruined the Tory Ogilvies into whom she married, Queen Victoria's postponed

Cortachy, a baronialized castle, Angus

visit saved Airlie, at least from being enlarged by Bryce or anyone else. Cortachy, on the other hand, was far from spared, for those who were 'born into the purple of commerce', to paraphrase Lady Bracknell, rather than 'risen from the ranks of the aristocracy', were very demanding, and more than thirty rooms were added to Cortachy by Bryce, plus a ballroom. Fortunately for later generations, most of this has been pulled down. Cortachy was used as a hospital during the last war and, not being cared for as it had been in the past, acquired dry rot, hence the demolitions; the mistaken enlargements were gratuitously removed to make a tolerable home for future earls and countesses of Airlie. Cortachy is a gay-looking building with little sense of antiquity, white harled with red sandstone here and there, Gothycke touches in its fase battlements, an amusing turreted round tower at one corner and the remnants of the original tower house at the other, domestic and unassuming.

Not far away in Inverquharity, from which Sir David Ogilvy at Winton takes his title. His ancestors abandoned it in the

Balbegno, Kincardineshire: a laird's tower with an eighteenth-century addition

eighteenth century to live near Dundee and then in this century went to Wintoun, though retaining the title. It is a splendid tower house of the fifteenth century which remained more or less intact except for the short arm in its L-plan which had crumbled away. This was built up recently in the form of a more modern house (but in keeping and using similar materials) by a retired colonial official and his wife.

Half the size of Airlie but very much in the same local-farmhouse style is the Georgian bit of Balbegno, just over the Kincardineshire border. The transformation here is on a small scale compared to some of the previous examples described but is nevertheless interesting. The sixteenth-century L-shaped tower house of the Wood family is today squeezed in between a seventeenth-century addition to the south and the charming madder-hued farmhouse to the north, with rooms from each merging at different points. The principal feature of Balbegno has been referred to earlier; it is the stone vaulted ceiling to the

Tyninghame House, East Lothian: a seventeenth-century nucleus
encased in nineteenth-century Jacobean

first-floor hall, decorated with painted armorial devices of the
main Scottish baronial families. It is no more medieval than the
sculptured Gothic hall at Towie Barclay but is a Jacobean
replacement of the more common timber flooring of olden days.
Above, on the second floor, are four bedrooms, each with its own
garderobe, which shows how up-to-date some of these lairds'
houses were, while above that the 'battlements' are broken by
false windows, with sculptured dummies leaning out. There are
also gun-loops and Renaissance roundels such as one finds at
Myres and Monimail, in Fife. The date is given as 1569, and the
initials of 'I. Wod' recall the family who acquired the barony from
James IV in 1498. A lovely view unfolds from the top over
surrounding fields and woods, and of the fine, gabled doocot
belonging to the property, which is now Sir William Gladstone's.

The beautiful red sandstone house which is the East Lothian
seat of the Earl of Haddington might, perhaps, have been
included in my first chapter, since the barony of which it is the

caput was part of the domains of the archbishops of St Andrews before the Reformation, and in the garden is one of the finest ruined chapels in the country, Romanesque and dedicated to the local St Baldred. However, Tyninghame House as one sees it today was almost wholly the creation of William Burn—indeed, it may be his happiest work in nineteenth-century Jacobean. It is certainly helped by the warm colour of the stonework which entirely encases, though it does not eliminate, a genuine Jacobean manor house erected by the first Earl. Behind the whimpled turrets, diagonally placed chimneystalks, little balconies, amusing strapwork and typical bay windows, the form of another building enclosing three sides of a courtyard remains, with a few exposed morsels surviving near the stables. Inside, Lady Haddington's good taste has seen to it that Burn's designs have also survived, the dark van Dyck brown-stained woodwork contrasting splendidly with her orange walls and other attractive backgrounds.

The lairds of Tyninghame, who came to East Lothian from Prestonfield in the sixteenth century, before the Dicks acquired that Edinburgh property, were a branch of the Hamiltons but added Baillie to their name when they married into that family from Mellerstain, in Berwickshire. The Hamiltons were a particularly distinguished and interesting family, one of the most interesting being John, brother of Sir Thomas Hamilton of Prestonfield, who was a clerk in Holy Orders and, remaining true to the Papacy, left the country to study law in Paris, where he rose first to become Professor of Philosophy and finally Rector of the University. Sir Thomas stayed at home and became a Law Lord there, while his son, the first Earl of Haddington and builder of Tyninghame, occupied a number of important posts under James VI and I, including those of Lord-Clerk Register of Scotland and Secretary of State. His descendant, the sixth Earl, Hereditary Keeper of Holyrood Park, was the laird responsible for the famous Tyninghame woods, which go right down to the sea and cover an otherwise desolate site, proving, as Sir Walter Scott later pointed out, that Scotland need not be the depressing land it is sometimes made out to be. He did this in the early eighteenth century, when conditions were not good for the country, thus acting as a true baron, as did the creator of Tyninghame House when he contemporaneously laid out the model village at its

Castle of Mey, formerly Barrogill: Gothic lodge

gates, all in the same red stone except one newer addition of this century, which is harled!

William Burn was very prolific and was employed far and wide, as far north as Caithness, in fact, by the Sinclair owners of Barrogill, since renamed the Castle of Mey. This rather straggling building had originally been less so and served as a fortified barn of the bishops of Caithness, some of the largish gun-loops with which they guarded their tiends (tithes) still being visible on the main elevation. It subsequently fell to the Sinclair earls of Caithness, who turned it into a typical tower of defence, Z in plan, with conically capped corner turrets (bartisans) and the huge kitchen chimney which is such a feature of the seaward and eastern elevations. In the nineteenth century William Burn was engaged in producing a building which Miss Sinclair of Caithness later described as 'possessing all the natural elegance of a house in London and all the external dignity of an ancient Highland residence'. Caithness, of course, is not Highland; it is Lowland Scotland beyond the Highlands, somewhat like Pembrokeshire

Queen Mother's garden, Castle of Mey

in respect of Wales. The speech and accent are Northumbrian English as it once was from the Humber to the Pentland Firth, and its lairds alternated between barons of genuine Norman descent and barons of an earlier Norse descent, all Scandinavian originally.

Burn tidied up the plan, moved the entrance from the north to the south, where he made a Tudor porch, raised the roofline, adding dormers, and lopped off the conical roofs from the corner turrets, which he also raised and provided with battlemented tops. There had been an anti-Napoleonic battery in the vicinity, the remnants of which can still be seen, and this may, possibly, have inspired the quasi-military aspect now given to old Barrogill. It also applied to the crenellated gazebo at the far corner of the walled garden, where fruit trees, vegetables and flowers flourish between large protecting Caithness slates in quite a remarkable way. Inside, the London residence aspect of Miss Sinclair's comments seems more apposite, though in practice it is really an Edinburgh 'New Town' residence, judging by most of the fittings, including the handsome Georgian chimneypieces.

This is HM Queen Elizabeth the Queen Mother's northern retreat, which she saved from demolition in the year following the death of the King. She was most particular about how it should be restored and would not let the purists have their way

Barrogill, or the Castle of Mey, Caithness, from the north

too much, especially in such things as glazing bars and differences in architectural style. After all, the Castle of Mey, as Barrogill now became, grew as we all grow; it was not ashamed of its age, its imperfections and variabilities, and Her Majesty wished it to remain so. Her own new wing, containing dining-room above and kitchen below, was influenced in its design by both the ancient tower of the Sinclair lairds and the newer work of William Burn, the principal decoration being her coat of arms carved by Hew Lorimer over the window. Everything was done in stone similar to the original, and the glazing bars all remained as they had been, either thick or thin, Gothic or Georgian, and not wrenched out and made uniform. She drew the expert's attention to the difference between the size and type of the astragals in the Adam dining-room at Holyrood and those elsewhere in the palace, remarking that no one had ever suggested making them all the same; referring to building in general, she repeated the words of a Wick joiner: 'If it looks right, it is right.'

With Barrogill the Sinclairs held the barony of Freswick, near Wick, but they gave it up in the fifteenth century to the Mowats of Buchollie, a property in Aberdeenshire. The Mowats built the existing Freswick House, though there was an old castle on the northern side of Freswick Bay which they renamed Buchollie when they first came. The site is, for Caithness, a sheltered one, the land falling down to the sea gently but enough to protect the bay from westerly winds, which here, as almost everywhere else in Scotland, dominate. There are no trees, but one could live at Freswick and not feel either too isolated or blown about. The wind is actually worse at the Castle of Mey, where, in order to get a few sycamores to grow, raspberry canes were planted around the young shoots, and constant clipping of the trees keeps them bushy and close together. The same was done at Ackergill, slightly nearer to Wick than Freswick, where the drive is lined by a rather moth-eaten-looking avenue which is so bedraggled one almost wishes the trees had never been planted. Ackergill was another Sinclair abode but much more exposed than almost any of the others. It was greatly restored by David Bryce and boasts two very fine, tall doocots which are original. It is the seat of Madam Dunbar of Hempriggs, that being the name of the barony.

Freswick boasts no doocots, no turrets, no battlements, nothing remotely baronial looking; it stands three storeys high, without adornment, its plain harled walls topped by ordinary domestic crow-stepped gables. It was bought recently and turned into a luxury hotel, the barony title being bought with it. The proprietor then returned to the south of England, sold the house and has since offered the barony title for sale as a separate item. I am told this might cost as much as £10,000, and one cynic has added that a book such as this one could put up the price by as much as double that figure. It will be a sad day if this does happen, for to possess the title to a feudal barony without its *caput*, and without being accounted 'amongst the noblesse of Scotland', to quote the wording on the grant of arms to such a baron, destroys the essential link between baron and barony. For, even if the barons no longer administer justice on behalf of the king, they still have their place in society when they occupy ancient baronial property and bear the arms appertaining to that property. In England they may do what they like, selling squire-doms and lordship of manors which exist only on paper, but on the Continent no title is accepted by the *Almanach de Gotha* unless associated with some land, however minute; hopefully this is how things will remain in Scotland.

Neither William Burn nor David Bryce had anything to do with

Craufurdland Castle, Fenwick, Ayrshire

Craufurdland Castle, near Fenwick, in Ayrshire, though one might have thought they had, judging by its Gothic frontispiece, false arrow-slits and over-large battlements. In fact, it was designed by the laird himself, a descendant of Sir Reginald Craufurd, Sheriff of Ayrshire, who acquired the barony in the thirteenth century, in the reign of Alexander II. The founder of the family and house was himself said to be the grandson of a descendant of Thorlongus, an Anglo-Danish chief from Northumberland. Perhaps that explains the present somewhat over-romantic appearance of the castle which, as elsewhere, actually hides an older laird's tower which is at present rented out by the family, who reside in the newer part. Some friends of mine were tenants and enjoyed being there very much, for at that time they had the place to themselves, farmed the land and played the laird, sending cattle to the shows and even occupying the baronial loft in Fenwick kirk. They also pulled off the ivy

Abbotsford, Roxburghshire

which still covered much of the structure when I sketched it, and which, in Victorian eyes, gave the place an authentically ancient look.

One of the Craufurds fell at Flodden and another was secretary successively to Mary of Guise and her daughter, Mary, Queen of Scots, who probably stayed at Craufurdland. In the eighteenth century the laird was a strong Jacobite and acted as valet to the condemned Earl of Kilmarnock when he went to his death at Tyburn, graciously spared the horrors of being hanged, drawn and quartered, being merely beheaded. The male line died out in the nineteenth century, when the castle was baronialized by John Howieson of Braehead, who married the heiress, thus uniting two old families, one from the west of Scotland, the other from the east. Braehead is near Cramond, on the outskirts of Edinburgh, and the barony was granted to one Jock Howieson in the sixteenth century by James V. That King liked to travel incognito amongst his people, no doubt to hear what they were saying, and was known to them as 'the Guidman o' Ballengeich'.

He was set upon by brigands on one occasion, Jock Howieson rescuing him and taking him into his house. From this episode derives the Howieson reddendo, to offer the sovereign a towel and ewer of water whenever he or she comes to Braehead.

Of course, the precursor of all Scots baronial houses of nineteenth century was Sir Walter Scott's Abbotsford, upon which a number of people worked, including John Atkinson, who had been employed by the Earl of Mansfield at Scone Palace; Edward Blore, a romantic like Scott himself; George Bullock, who did the interiors; and Sir Walter, who got out of the others what he wanted and added his own peculiar touches wherever he thought necessary. Abbotsford was not a barony; it started with a few acres purchased from the local minister and called by the unpromising name of Clartey Hole. To this the author of *Waverley* added hundreds of acres, bit by bit, planting woods and making a most attractive park beside the Tweed, his native river. Although ostensibly Scots, Sir Walter called Abbotsford 'an English manor house', and had he also been the master of personal propaganda, like William Beckwith of Fonthill or Horace Walpole of Strawberry Hill, his house would not only have had an immediate effect on contemporary architectural taste but become a principal source of material for researchers in our own day, instead of being passed over as dull and even stereotyped by comparison. It was completely misunderstood in its begetter's lifetime, considered little better than a whim, and an expensive one at that, of the great man, who was the foremost author of his age and the veritable inventor of the historical novel as it has come down to us via the pens of Alexandre Dumas, *père et fils*, and Victor Hugo.

His literary proclivities, plus his amusing if harmless *folies de grandeur* all went into the creation of Abbotsford; Ruskin may have been disappointed by it, Queen Victoria likewise, but they saw it after it had acquired many imitators and all of them the work of more effusive if inferior literary or artistic personages. Scott's weakness shows not so much in an exterior composed of features from all over the place, the door and doorway from Edinburgh's Tolbooth, or ancient prison, which was pulled down whilst Abbotsford was a building, the entrance to Linlithgow Palace, which he had copied for his own house, a turreted tower from ruined Melrose and above all the crow-stepped replica of

Darnick, which he admired and coveted, but in the interior, which is a squirrel-like collection of armour and books, curiosities and intimate souvenirs of the famous and infamous. He was one of the first civilians allowed on the Field of Waterloo, and so there is a Napoleonic cuirass and sword, even the blotter and pen used by Bonaparte which fell from his coach; these, with the key from Loch Leven Castle, erstwhile prison of Mary, Queen of Scots, Bonnie Prince Charlie's hunting knives, Rob Roy's sporran and a lock of Nelson's hair, are more or less lumped together.

'The Bard of Abbotsford' was very much a man of his time, the confidant of kings and princes, a strong Tory and the writer who made it his business to collect his country's legends and tell its story before it was finally merged into the wider nationalism of Great Britain herself. He was a considerable friend of George IV, being the first baronet created in the reign of that theatrical monarch who, as Scott himself declared, could be accepted by all patriotic Scots as their king since he did not come to the throne until after the death of the last Stuart, Cardinal York, in 1807.

Scott's love of pageantry and heraldry and his desire to play the country gentleman are evident in the hall, with its ceiling covered with coats of arms showing his own Scott connections. Unfortunately his mother's side is not represented, she having no arms, which must have been a disappointment to the would-be laird and baron. He was loved by everyone, and no one more so than those who came under his jurisdiction as 'shirra' (sheriff) of Selkirk, where he administered justice so benignly and fairly that minor miscreants must almost have looked forward to being brought before him. He loved the homily that went with sentence and is one of the very few sheriffs whose statue stands honoured outside the court where he functioned. Scott liked to think he combined in his personality and attitudes the patriarchal Celtic side and the feudal, the former with its historical allegiances, the latter with its sense of law and order. There is a picture by Sir David Wilkie showing Sir Walter, his family and servants in rustic state, the Bard wearing an old hat, holding a nobbly stick, at his feet a 'tappit hen' (a quart ale pot); to his left stands Sir Adam Ferguson, his factor, while to his right his daughter carries a wooden milk pail on her head; his French wife, Charlotte, is beyond, and looking soulfully at his master is the ever faithful deerhound. This describes one side of the laird of Abbotsford.

William Allan's *Gala Day at Abbotsford* shows something else. It is a description in paint, albeit unfinished, of the whole, generous, cosmopolitan spirit of the Romantic Age itself, with at its centre the genius who presided over it. For here, beneath the shadow of 'Gothycke' Abbotsford, with umbrella held aloft by a

Balmoral, an original castle much enlarged

servant, sits Sir Walter Scott, Bart., his right hand fondling his deerhound, acknowledging quite naturally, without any embarrassment, the homage, indeed adulation, of a clientele of country riders, gentry and fellow lairds, of society ladies, poets and painters and the merely curious. No other Scotsman in his own lifetime has ever risen to such a height of international fame nor been so genuinely loved and respected by all and sundry. Yet Abbotsford itself, the scene of this apotheosis-like vision, has not received much attention, far less praise, though, apart from some additions made for Scott's descendants by William Burn, it was largely the creation of the man who rejoiced under the nickname of 'Duke of Darnick'.

Of course, Abbotsford does have its imitations, but they are less important than the general effect and influence of the life led there by its celebrated laird. One recalls a delightful *manoir* in Normandy which was almost ruined by the *seigneur* wishing to emulate Scott's example, adding parapets, battlements and turrets to the traditionally high, sloping roof of his ancient seat and thus making problems for his successors, who have suffered from the rain getting in ever since! Perhaps Balmoral alone of the larger and better-known baronial piles of the nineteenth century can be said to be directly inspired by Abbotsford, and there too, the laird, Prince Albert, was at least half his own architect, leaning heavily on the Aberdonian William Smith. Scott actually had three architects at his elbow, while remaining the chief one himself, designing the handsome arcade dividing the garden from the entrance court without assistance from anyone. Though a baronet and a laird, he had no red *chapeau* and Abbotsford was not the seat of a feudal barony. Yet it would be ungracious not to accord him honorary feudal baron status, for it was surely here, on the banks of the Tweed, that the spirit, if not the letter, of feudalism was revived and epitomized in a way never repeated, not even by Victoria and Albert in their idyll on the banks of the Dee.

Basically the feudal system has survived intact and viable, especially where the question of land tenure is concerned. In 1914 the Feudal Casualties (Scotland) Act abolished additional payments due to a superior on the occurrence of specified events, such as the death of a vassal.

A more concentrated attempt to modify, if not totally abolish, the whole system failed in 1972, when the Scottish Home and Health Department, acting no doubt under current political pressures, put out a Green Paper on the subject. Contradictory in character, it contained in item 16 the following somewhat contentious statement that modification, as opposed to abolition, 'would inevitably leave intact the framework of a system of complex multi-tier ownership of land which is unacceptable on social grounds in the latter part of the Twentieth century'. What those 'social grounds' are is not stated or at all substantiated in the rest of the document, which begins by confirming that, 'Most land in Scotland is still held on one form or another of feudal tenure, a system dating from the eleventh and twelfth centuries.' It would appear from this that the longevity of the system is in itself to be deprecated. In item 14, however, the Green Paper seems to retreat slightly and give qualified support for the feudal system; thus: 'The Feudal System has in practice proved able to accommodate most forms of land use and development. It has provided a simple mechanism for establishing conditions to run with land, many of which have been beneficial in their effect. The fact that the proprietor of land which is feud can hold it in perpetuity, subject always to payment of feuduty and the observance of any land condition, means that he has security of tenure; and, this being so, the Feudal System does not give rise to the type of social problem which can occur, for example, at the termination of a long lease.' One senses here the more clear-headed approach of Scottish lawyers and permanent officials whose knowledge of affairs north of the Border is greater than their fear of losing political kudos.

The 1748 Heritable Jurisdiction Act, which began the controversy, did reduce the power of the feudal barons, at least in respect of capital crimes and their punishment, but, as the present Lord Lyon himself has pointed out, by comparison with the rights of barons elsewhere, and particularly on the Continent, 'They are magnificent.' The Act was quite clear on a number of interesting points, such as the maximum fines that could be imposed and where and how any imprisonment would be effected, even down to the fine to be imposed on any baron not complying with its terms. It is written in Gothic script and the language is archaic in places, yet it is precise and forthright in its details and still represents the law of the land. Indeed, if one wishes to dispose of the idea that the feudal system was abolished in Scotland by it, a brief perusal is all that is needed to show that the Act of 1748, far from abolishing the system actually strengthened it in some respects. It removed practices that had long since been discontinued or fallen into disuse, while confirming the barons' rights and privileges in other directions.

It seems to me that anything that works, and does so reasonably well, should be maintained, and things that do not should be scrapped and replaced. The British Monarchy is surely in the first category: it does work and has survived largely because it has been able to adapt itself to changing conditions down the ages. The monarchy is the fountain of honour and stands at the head of the feudal system, which in England, at any rate, seems to have failed where the monarchy has succeeded, while it survives in Scotland. What applies to the system must surely be true of its outward and visible signs, not only in the matter of land tenure, the bearing of arms and continuity of certain privileges but in the preservation or otherwise of baronial property. If it remains in the hands of the feudal baron, that is one thing, but what if he must sell and it goes to the National Trust, or even to some less culturally interested party? Most people, I'm sure, would like to think when they visit a property of historical and architectural value that it still houses a laird or his dame, however infrequently. In France they set great store by the presence of the *propriétaire actuelle*, whether merely in a signed photograph or more tangibly in a newly stubbed out cigarette in the salon. I think too that, even if a baronial house has to be sold and even if a well-meaning public body acquires it, the presence of perfectly arranged flowers in the rooms is not enough, and especially not furniture arranged to suit the taste of some professional interior decorator. The main rooms should be left more or less as the last proprietor had them, down to any books and possibly out-of-date 'modern' chairs and tables that were there, not forgetting a few ancient photographs. I've seen a stuffed dog half-way up the stairs as well, and not a bad touch either.

The building and its more obvious treasures may be saved for posterity by a judicious sale to the National Trust, but turning someone's home, the home perhaps of generations, into a museum should be avoided as much as possible. A caring tenant would seem to be the answer. They apparently do something like this in a few Communist countries, where the ancestral family are occasionally permitted to stay as guardians and caretakers. Gardens also must be protected from over-zealous gardeners whose main interest is tidying everything up. They rarely display the same love for plants as the former owners. How this can be done is a moot point, but now that so many properties have been taken over is the time to start thinking seriously about it, before the gardens resemble those in municipal parks and before the buildings look as if the Works Department had been busy on them.

I recently visited the Palace of Holyroodhouse, and wished I hadn't. Ostensibly royal property, someone has got over the hurdle of royal approval and the place has become a virtual void—the historical apartments, I mean, not the rooms occupied either by the Duke of Hamilton, who is the official Keeper, or by Her Majesty the Queen and the Court, which are, presumably, inviolate. Queen Mary's bed has gone, no one knows where or will say, and so has almost everything else one had associated with the place. These objects may not all have been genuine—certainly the bed did not belong to Mary, Queen of Scots, but it probably did to Mary of Modena, consort of James VII and II, who stayed here in the seventeenth century, but those terrible empty rooms, with spotlights spotting very little, and the gloom, are depressing in the extreme. One hardly supposes this was intended, even though the place has had a sad history.

It is the grinding 'authenticity' that most depresses and which is far from convincing in any case. Evolution is what really matters, and if a building has evolved in a certain manner, then that is its authenticity, and the removal of culturally annoying items by the fastidious is not. A great deal more education is clearly needed if we are to control the activities of self-styled experts and others anxious to improve us and our inherited cultured environment. We must at all costs retain more of the human qualities inherent in our architecturally interesting and historically valuable buildings, and be able to relate them to the institutions and persons who built them or who may still be associated with them.

Open to the Public

Most of the houses described and illustrated in this book are private and in consequence are not regularly, if at all, open to the public. There are, of course, special problems for owners opening to visitors, problems of insurance, rating and maintenance which are worth facing only if opening is on a large scale, as in the case of the more famous country houses and castles of Britain. However, a number of interesting *caputs* of baronies can be seen when they are open under Scotland's Gardens Scheme, when, even if the whole house is not visible, the exterior is, and probably part of the interior, where tea may often be taken. These openings are variable but the organizer of Scotland's Gardens Scheme will be pleased to supply information if enquirers write to him at 26 Castle Terrace, Edinburgh EHI The Scottish Tourist Board, at 23 Ravelston Terrace, Edinburgh EH4, publishes a list of most properties open to the public, which includes a number of those described. Ancient Monuments, Scottish Division, at 3–11 Melville Street, Edinburgh EH3, will also supply information on properties under their control, including Duff House, Banff; Hailes Castle, East Lothian; Huntingtower, Perthshire; Huntly Castle, Aberdeenshire; Kinneil House, West Lothian; Scotstarvit Tower, Fife, and Spynie Palace, Moray, all of which have their place in the story of Scotland's historic baronies. Finally, the National Trust for Scotland, 5 Charlotte Square, Edinburgh EH2, have in their care the following important baronial houses: the House of the Binns, Brodie, Craigievar, Crathes, Drum Castle, Fyvie, Leith Hall, Magdalen House, Pitmedden (The Great Garden), Provan Hall and Hill of Tarvit, which are open throughout most of the year, except for Provan Hall, which can be seen externally, however; Magdalen, which is let but again can easily be seen from outside; and Hill of Tarvit, only part of which is open to visitors, the rest being divided into flats.

Bibliography

The Antiquities of Scotland, R. W. Billings, in four volumes (1852)

Castellated and Domestic Architecture of Scotland, MacGibbon and Ross, Volumes I & II (1886)

Scottish Homes and Shrines, Sir John Stirling Maxwell, Bt (Chambers, 1938)

The Stones of Scotland, edited by G. S. Moncrieffe (Batsford, 1938)

Scottish Castles of the 16th and 17th Centuries, Oliver Hill (*Country Life*, 1953)

Scottish Country Houses and Gardens Open to the Public, J. Fleming (*Country Life*, 1954)

The Historic Architecture of Scotland, J. Dunbar (Batsford, 1966)

Architect Royal Life and Works of Sir Wm. Bruce, Hubert Fenwick (Roundwood, 1970)

Scotland's Historic Buildings, Hubert Fenwick (Hale, 1974)

The Gothic Revival, J. Macaulay (Blackie, 1975)

Scotland's Castles, Hubert Fenwick (Hale, 1976)

The Buildings of Scotland: The Lothians, N. Pevsner, edited by C. McWilliam (Penguin, 1978)

Inventories of the Royal Commission on Ancient Monuments in Scotland

Glossary

ASHLAR: Dressed stone
ASTRAGAL: Glazing bar
AUMBRY: Wall cupboard

BARMKIN: Outer defence wall
BARREL-VAULT: Semi-circular roof of stone or timber
BARTISAN: Battlemented sentry post
BELLCAST: Hipped roof, upturned at eaves
BOSS: Covering at junction of vaulting
BRETÈCHE: Look-out with space for dropping detergents on
    unwanted visitors

CAP-HOUSE: Small building opening onto roof
CARYATID: Support in form of human effigy
CLOSE: Building with courtyard
CORBEL: Projection in stone or timber giving structural support
CROW-STEPS: Stepped gable ends
CRENELLATION: Indentation of battlements

DONJON: Keep of Norman castle
DOOCOT: Dovecote, circular or rectangular, and when domed
    known as 'beehive'
DYKE: Stone wall

ENCEINTE: Enclosing wall of medieval castle

FORESTAIRS: External stairs of wood or stone
FOSSE: Ditch or moat, dry or wet
FURCA: Fork in tree for hanging miscreants

GARDEROBE: Closet or lavatory
GAZEBO: Garden house

GROIN: Junction in vaulting

HARLING: Sand, lime and ballast rendering to rough masonry

JAMB: Support to doorway or wndow
JOUGS: Metal neckpiece for wrong-doers

LAICH: Low or lower hall

MACHICOLATIONS: Corbelled supports to parapet
MOTTE: Mound, often artificial, upon which fort or castle stood

NEWEL: Support for staircase

OGEE: Shape in which convex and concave curves combine
OVERSAILING: Lean-to roof replacing conical cap to tower or
    turret

PALAS: Place; long building as opposed to tall
PALLADIAN: Style based on Roman introduced by Andrea
    Palladio in sixteenth century
PELE: Wooden palisade, later a tower of stone
PEND: Vaulted passage
PERRON: External steps at entrance to building
PORT: Entrance gateway to medieval burgh

QUOIN: Cornerstone (BUCKLE-QUOIN: in shape of buckle)

ROMANESQUE: Buildings derived from Roman and
    characterized by rounded arches

SCALE-AND-PLATT: Straight stair with landings
SHOT-HOLE: Hole for use of firearms
SHUT-HOLE: Hole that can be opened or closed for ventilation
SHUTTER-BOARD WINDOW: Window with fixed upper lights
    and opening wooden shutter below
SKEW-PUTT: Finish to skew, or gable coping at eaves
SOLAR: Lord's upper hall or private room
STUDY: Small room in turret
SWEPT-DORMER: Dormer window with swept-up roof

TURNPIKE STAIR: Spiral staircase

WYND: Narrow passage between houses

YETT: Iron grille or gate

NB The above glossary is based on those provided in my *Scotland's Historic Buildings,* and *Scotland's Castles.*

Index